Illustrated
STORIES from the
BOOK of MORMON

Illustrated
STORIES from the BOOK of MORMON

Volume 4

Dr. Clinton F. Larson, *Narrative and Editing*
Professor of English, Brigham Young University

Joseph N. Revill, *Correlator and Writer; Associate Editor*

Stuart Heimdal, *Artist and Art Director*

Dr. Paul Cheesman, *Director of Research*

Published by
PROMISED LAND PUBLICATIONS, INC.
Provo, Utah

FIRST EDITION VOLUME 4 1969

Lithographed in U.S.A.
PROMISED LAND PRESS
Provo, Utah

Contents

Foreword

<blockquote>
"... give ear unto my words; for because the words of Isaiah are not plain unto you, nevertheless they are plain unto all those that are filled with the spirit of prophecy ... Yea, and my soul delighteth in the words of Isaiah ..."
</blockquote>

2 Nephi 25:4-5

As we approach the momentous task of illustrating the 2nd Book of Nephi, we can but hope and pray that the spirit may be operative in our behalf as well as in the minds and hearts of our readers. This volume contains many of the writings of Isaiah, that brilliant prophet of Israel. It is necessary, as Nephi said, that one have the proper spirit to understand and appreciate these inspired phrases.

We are hopeful that our efforts here will aid in gaining an appreciation of the message Isaiah had for both ancient Israel and for us today.

— *The Publishers*

Acknowledgments

Again we must acknowledge the efforts of a great number of people, who have been working in harmony and often at great sacrifice to prepare Volume 4 of *Illustrated Stories from the Book of Mormon.*

We are especially fortunate to have the services of Dr. Paul R. Cheesman of Brigham Young University who has been appointed Director of Research for Promised Land Publications, Inc. Dr. Cheesman has a wide background in Book of Mormon research. He has made numerous visits to Central and South America, where so many ancient ruins are evidence of the Book of Mormon culture and period. We are confident that Dr. Cheesman's work with us will bring to our readers authentic portrayals of this historic period.

We must here acknowledge a great appreciation on our part for the untiring efforts of Dr. Sidney B. Sperry and Dr. Ellis T. Rasmussen. Without the help of these brilliant scholars it would have been more difficult if not impossible to interpret and illustrate Isaiah as we have done here. The years of research and study behind the efforts of these two men, and the spirit they carry to share this knowledge with all of us, make our hearts glad to be associated with them.

Again we want to express a deep appreciation to Dr. Clinton F. Larson for his masterful handling of the narrative accompanying each of the illustrations. We feel that Dr. Larson has captured the spirit and meaning that Isaiah had in mind when he wrote his message. To interpret this and condense it into our modern phrases of expression, on a level that all ages can read and understand is a rare gift and one Dr. Larson possesses.

We are most fortunate to have the services of a new art director in Promised Land Publications, Inc., whose work we deeply appreciate. Stuart Heimdal has recently been appointed to this important responsibility. The duties associated with this position require a constant vigilance to direct, create, or have created, all of the illustrations in these publications. These art pieces must meet exacting requirements for authenticity and reality.

Mr. Heimdal's extensive experience in addition to a Master's degree in art from Brigham Young University, certainly qualifies him for this assignment.

Our schedule of production of subsequent volumes of *Illustrated Stories from the Book of Mormon* will be greatly aided and benefited by this change in our art department. Mr. Heimdal has been greatly aided in his work by Vernon Murdock, Jon Anderson, Stan Russon and Bob Reese, to whom we give grateful appreciation for their efforts in this volume.

To the entire advisory board who has labored long and hard in the preparation of this volume, we give our appreciation. These men are Dr. Sidney B. Sperry, Dr. Ellis T. Rasmussen, Dr. Ross T. Christensen, Dr. Clinton F. Larson, Golden Berrett, Dr. Paul R. Cheesman, and Joseph N. Revill, Chairman and Correlator of the material.

— *The Publishers*

A Short History of The Church of Jesus Christ of Latter-day Saints

CHAPTER 4

by Joseph N. Revill

The new little Church, with a hundred enemies for each friend, was now ready to fulfill the Lord's decree, "Go ye unto all the world and preach the Gospel."

In June, 1830, the Prophet Joseph Smith called his brother Samuel to be one of the first missionaries for the Church. Equipped with a number of copies of the Book of Mormon, he set out on a journey to visit locations in western New York.

To Samuel, his work may have seemed fruitless — yet the contacts he made and the copies of the Book of Mormon he distributed were directly responsible for bringing personalities into the Church who have changed and influenced the course of history in this nation.

One copy of the Book of Mormon left with Rev. John P. Greene, a Methodist minister, was placed in the hands of the Young and Kimball families. This ultimately brought Brigham Young, Heber C. Kimball and many members of their families into the Church. These two personalities were to play prominent roles in the history of the Church and the colonization of the West.

Other missionary efforts by the Prophet's father and other brothers were productive, and the Church converted many seeking the truth. Very rapidly the membership expanded and soon passed one hundred.

Other copies of this book found their way to men who were to become prominent in history. Parley P. Pratt, who was preaching what was known as Campbellism, a new religious movement of the time,

read the Book of Mormon, joined the Church and straightaway was instrumental in bringing his brother Orson into the fold.

While nearly every member was engaged in missionary effort, the Lord kept the Prophet busy with new revelation, and here a little, there a little added to strengthen the restored Church.

During this time the Prophet received a revelation on the details of the Lord's communication and instruction to Moses, which had long been lost to the world. These can now be found in the Pearl of Great Price. A revelation was received about this time on the procedure and importance of the sacrament of the Lord's Supper.

While the growth and progress were greatly encouraging — not all was right. Lucifer was busy stirring up trouble and trying to thwart the work of the Lord. Great enmity existed in Colesville, N. Y., where a branch of the Church had flourished. Some of the early baptisms performed there brought mob violence and resulted in the arrest of Joseph Smith on false charges. He was tried twice and acquitted of these charges.

At the second general conference of the Church, held September 26, 1830, at Fayette, New York, the first mission to the Lamanites was appointed through revelation. Oliver Cowdery, Ziba Peterson, Peter Whitmer, Jr., and Parley P. Pratt were called to take the Book of Mormon to the Indian tribes in the West. As the four missionaries traveled westward, they preached the gospel on every occasion. They visited the Catteraugus Indians near Buffalo, New York, and left the Book of Mormon with them.

As they journeyed westward into Ohio, where Parley P. Pratt had lived, they worked among the scattered population around Mentor and Kirtland, where Sidney Rigdon was a preacher with the Disciples or Campbellite Movement. Here they converted Rigdon and many of his congregation. Though there was some bitterness in the area, branches of the Church were organized and the membership grew. In the area of Sandusky, Ohio, they preached to the Wyandot Indians and left them copies of the Book of Mormon.

Traveling down the Ohio River to its mouth on the Mississippi; the missionaries found the river blocked with ice and were required to press westward to St. Louis and on to Independence, Missouri, by foot. Independence was then only a trading post on the Western boundaries of the United States.

The missionaries preached the gospel to the Delaware Indians and were joyously received until certain

Indian agents and sectarian missionaries objected. They threatened to bring military interference if the missionaries continued their preaching.

Opposition and persecution continued to mount against the Church in New York. The Lord directed that the members move to Ohio, as enemies were planning their destruction. Gradually and without haste, as the Lord had directed, the members moved to the Kirtland, Ohio area, the Colesville Branch settling at Thompson.

The Lord continued to pour out knowledge and direction through his Prophet Joseph. He made many things known concerning his second coming and the signs of the times in preparing his people for the trials and tribulations they would endure in establishing Zion.

He had made known that they would move again when the city of Zion was to be established. Where this was to be, he was not ready to make known, but it was to be somewhere in the West.

At the June, 1831, conference in Kirtland, the first high priests in this dispensation were ordained. The Church now numbered more than a thousand members. At this conference the Lord revealed that the city of Zion was to be located in the land of Missouri. The saints were to gather gradually there, and if they were faithful they would possess it as a land of inheritance.

Many elders were called to go two by two, preaching as they traveled westward until they would all assemble in Jackson County, Missouri, where the next conference would be held. The exact location of the city of Zion with its house of the Lord would be made known to them at their journey's end.

With the arrival in Missouri of the leading elders of the Church, the Lord made known that the city of Zion was to be located at Independence, with the temple to be located a little west of the courthouse. Direction was given that the saints were to purchase all of the lands available and although the future glory of Zion was yet distant, many of them felt the time had arrived for permanent settlement.

On August 3, 1831, the site for the building of the great temple of the latter days was dedicated. Here was to be the center of the holy city spoken of by ancient seers from whence the law should go forth to the ends of the earth.

Revelation continued to flow to the saints through the Prophet, and direction was given that these commandments and revelations should be published and printed on a press to be established in Zion. During this period, Joseph Smith and Sidney Rigdon were given a vision of the glories of the kingdom of heaven. This choice revelation is contained in Section 76 of the Doctrine and Covenants.

On March 24, 1832 — while the Prophet and Sidney Rigdon, who was acting as a scribe for him were engaged in revising the scriptures, under inspiration of the Spirit, at Hiram, Ohio — mob violence broke out, and Joseph and Sidney were beaten nearly to death. They were then taken stripped of their clothes, and a coat of tar and feathers was applied to their bodies. Thus Lucifer continued his efforts through men of evil design to impede the progress of truth.

Many other important revelations were given during this period and are now sections of the Doctrine and Covenants.

The gospel net continued to draw in many converts who were to play important parts in the history of the Church in years to come. It was about November 8, 1832, that Brigham Young, Heber C. Kimball, and others first met the Prophet Joseph.

On March 18, 1833, the First Presidency was organized in compliance with a revelation given on the 8th of March (Sec. 90, D&C). Joseph Smith was placed as the head, with Sidney Rigdon and Frederick G. Williams as counselors.

In June, 1833, preparations for building a temple in Kirtland were under way. This was in compliance with previous revelations, that the elders could receive instruction necessary before going out to warn the world.

In Zion, meanwhile, not all was well with the saints. Mobs were being organized to drive the saints from Jackson County. Hatred had been stirred up by various ministers because of the religious beliefs of the Mormons. The mobs feared that the Mormons would get political domination, and they hated the industry of the saints.

The angry mob made formal demands that the Mormons move out of the county, peaceably if possible, but they would be forcibly moved if they refused the mob demands. They were not even given fifteen minutes to consider the demands. It did not matter that they had purchased their lands, that they were law-abiding citizens — their evils consisted in belief in visions, revelations, miracles and priesthood powers. These the mob could not tolerate.

Thus began five years of constant persecution, mobbings, robbings, house burnings, murderings, revilings of women, all with the sanction of the laws of a state government administered by cowardly, evil individuals. Any appeals from the saints to the governor were treated either with contempt or forgotten.

In bitter winter weather in early November, 1833, the mobs drove out some twelve hundred saints, burned their homes, beat the men, and forced women and children into the storms with little or no provisions. They crossed the Missouri River into Clay County where they were received with some degree of compassion.

Back in Kirtland the first high council was organized. Revelation was given as to procedure the Church was to follow respecting Zion. Volunteers were called for to make a march to Zion to help the exiled saints. This expedition became known as Zion's Camp. The march was made and although it did not accomplish all its intended motives, it proved to be a good training ground for many who later were called to responsible trusts in the Church. The Lord declared that had it not been for the transgressions of the saints they might have been redeemed even now. He advised that the march had been a test of the faith of the members.

Arbitration between the Jackson County mob and the saints now in Clay County came to no success and redress from the government was not forthcoming. The saints were denied possession of their rightful properties and now had to start anew.

For a season at least the opposition began to subside in Clay County and the saints began to make progress toward building up at least a part of Zion.

Membership continued to increase at a rapid rate.

In Kirtland on the 14th of February, 1835, all of the brethren who had been a part of Zion's Camp, who could be assembled, gathered and the first Quorum of the Twelve Apostles was called and organized. On the 28th of February the first Quorum of Seventy was organized.

So step by step, piece by piece the Lord was preparing his kingdom that all could be made ready for his second coming. Now his house being built in Kirtland, at great sacrifice on the part of the saints, was nearing completion.

On March 27, 1836, a great event occurred. The temple, the first house of the Lord built in this dispensation, was dedicated. Great and remarkable manifestations were given on this occasion and the saints were filled with the spirit.

Ordinance work immediately went forth in the temple and the Savior appeared to several of the brethren and angels ministered to others during these sessions.

On April 3, 1836, at a meeting in the temple Joseph Smith and Oliver Cowdery retired to the pulpit, the veils being drawn. After kneeling in silent prayer, they testified that the Savior appeared to them, standing on the breastwork of the pulpit. He blessed them and accepted the temple in his name.

After this vision closed the heavens opened again and Moses appeared, committing to them the keys of the gathering of Israel. Elias, who was a contemporary of Abraham, appeared and committed to them the keys of the dispensation of the Gospel of Abraham. This was followed by the appearance of Elijah, who Malachi said would be sent, turning the hearts of the fathers to the children and the hearts of the children to their fathers—before the coming of the Lord in the great and dreadful day.

The great progress the Church was making in spite of the opposition was too much for Lucifer. There he determined an all-out fight. From every quarter now his influence began to be felt. Even some of the saints, who had suffered themselves, began to find fault and to fail in their responsibilities to the Church and to criticize those in authority.

In Missouri the enemies in Jackson County, not content with the removal of the saints from their county, began putting pressure on the Clay County people to get rid of the Mormon menace from among them. To avoid further trouble, the saints agreed to the peaceful removal. They went into the north part of Ray County into an unsettled portion of the state. Near Shoal Creek they purchased lands and commenced to build their homes. Their petition to the state for a county organization was granted, and Caldwell County was established. By November, 1837, the Prophet was again in Missouri. In council with

the elders there it was decided that the city of Far West would be established as the center to which all of the saints would be encouraged to gather.

The seeds of apostasy had been planted among some of the leading brethren, and Lucifer was taking his toll. The Prophet said at this time that it seemed, "as though all the powers of earth and hell were combining their influence in an especial manner to overthrow the Church at once, and make a final end."

But there was one great ray of hope. The Spirit directed the Prophet to send Heber C. Kimball to Great Britain to carry the gospel to the people of that nation. Orson Hyde was set apart to accompany him on this mission.

Missionary work in Canada by Orson Pratt, Parley P. Pratt, and others had been successful in the past. In 1836, Parley P. Pratt had succeeded in bringing John Taylor, Joseph Fielding, and others into the Church, in the future history of which they were to play very important roles.

Joseph Fielding and Willard Richards were set apart to accompany Elders Kimball and Hyde on this mission. Arriving in England on July 20, 1837, this little band of missionaries commenced their labors at Preston, where Elder Fielding had a brother who

was a minister. This brother opened his chapel to the elders, and they had great success in their labors. Soon many people had joined the Church, and branches were established.

During these successes in England, things at Kirtland were going from bad to worse. It became necessary for Brigham Young to flee for his life because he continued publicly to testify that Joseph was a prophet and had not transgressed, as the apostates maintained. So strong were the feelings against the Prophet that he and Sidney Rigdon had to flee to Missouri in January, 1838.

In Missouri, the spirit of apostasy was taking its toll, and many of the prominent elders were deserting the fight. Transgression, fault-finding and refusal to acknowledge those in authority were the main causes of these apostasies. Among those to fall by the way were Oliver Cowdery and David Whitmer, both of whom were witnesses to the Book of Mormon. Both of these men were excommunicated but neither during his lifetime ever denied his testimony concerning the Book of Mormon.

Others to fall by the wayside during these trying times were Lyman Johnson, William E. McLellin, Jacob Whitmer, and Hiram Page. This was a sad day

for the Prophet to see so many of his former friends and fellow laborers become affected by the spirit of apostasy. Regardless of the bleakness of the situation, the Church continued to grow, and the saints gathered in great numbers to Far West and other places round about the region. Stakes were organized and a site was selected for building a house of the Lord at Far West.

By July, 1838, most of the remaining faithful saints in Kirtland, under the direction of the Seventies, commenced their journey to Zion, arriving at Adam-ondi-Ahman, some 25 miles north of Far West, on October 4, 1838.

Lucifer could not stand these successes in the face of the opposition he had mustered. The events which he influenced from here on to the final expulsion of these saints from Missouri will live in history as the darkest days in Missouri. The blood of these innocent people shall ever cry from the soil of that choice corner of this great nation.

Yes, mob violence was about to be loosed, the like of which had never before nor since occurred in the United States of America and gone unpunished and unredeemed.

Mobs began to gather, and with the aid and in-stigation of the governor, Lilburn W. Boggs, a series of mobbings, murderings, burnings, rapings, and all manner of persecution was loosed on these innocent people. We recount only one of many incidents which occurred at this time at Haun's Mill, a small settlement on Shoal Creek; some of the saints were peaceably going about their labors when, on October 30, 1838, a detachment of state troops attacked these defenseless citizens and shot men, women, and children, then robbed their lifeless bodies and their homes of any valuables, boasting of their deeds as though they were deeds of valor instead of shame. These men were acting under orders of the governor—the Mormons were to be exterminated or driven from the state. Under the same orders, state troops of over two thousand men were gathered to Far West to carry out this infamous, despicable order.

The surrender of their leaders and appropriation of their properties, the surrender of their arms and their explusion from the state were the only conditions that would forestall the mass execution of men, women, and children.

Joseph Smith, Sidney Rigdon, Parley P. Pratt, Lyman Wight, and George W. Robinson were to be surrendered as a ransom for the rest of the saints.

These men went willingly, and at a court martial during the night they were condemned to be shot in the public square the next morning.

Fortunately General Alexander W. Doniphan was given the order to carry out the execution, and he refused, calling it cold-blooded murder.

The prisoners were taken to Independence, and from there to Richmond, where they were kept in chains and abused. It was here the Prophet rebuked the guards by the power of the priesthood.

Their trial was held after much delay, and as witnesses came forth in their defense the witnesses were imprisoned.

The final outcome of the trial resulted in the Prophet, his brother Hyrum, Sidney Rigdon, Lyman Wight, Caleb Baldwin, and Alexander McRae being sent to Liberty, Clay County, Missouri, where they were confined for six months under very foul conditions.

It was only by the blessing of the Lord that they finally escaped and after much suffering made their way into Illinois.

During this period, the task of getting the exiled saints out of Missouri into Illinois fell to Brigham Young, for the First Presidency was in prison. Thus ended, until some future time, the abode of the saints in Missouri — they were now exiles on the soil of Illinois.

Moroni's Challenge

And when ye shall receive these things, I would exhort you that ye would ask God, the Eternal Father, in the name of Christ, if these things are not true; and if ye shall ask with a sincere heart, with real intent, having faith in Christ, he will manifest the truth of it unto you, by the power of the Holy Ghost. Moroni 10:4.

Portraits in Words

by Joseph N. Revill

"Ye have not chosen me, but I have chosen you, and ordained you, that ye should go and bring forth fruit, and that your fruit should remain: that whatsoever ye shall ask of the Father in my name, he may give it you.

"If the world hate you, ye know that it hated me before it hated you . . . I have chosen you out of the world, therefore the world hateth you . . . If they have persecuted me, they will also persecute you . . .

John 15:16-20

Although this quotation was spoken by the Savior Jesus Christ to his apostles just before his crucifixion, there is, however, a universal application of the principle of persecution.

Jesus had given these men the holy priesthood, by which they could act in the name of God and could command by this power, and as Jesus said, "He may give it you."

Some of these same apostles had appeared to Joseph Smith in 1829 and had given to him the same power and authority which they had received from the Christ. With this commission went also the same responsibility and same promise that the world would hate him and persecute him.

History amply attests that Joseph Smith, like Peter and the other apostles, was true to this endowment and never wavered nor faltered in his responsibility. Numerous incidents in his life demonstrated his fearless approach to his assignment.

After suffering along with many of the saints in the murderous and barbarous persecutions for over five years at the hands of mobs in Missouri, Joseph was taken prisoner along with other leaders of the Church, and for months they were kept in a dungeon prison in chains, awaiting trial on false charges.

Parley P. Pratt, one of the prisoners, recorded the following event:

"In one of those tedious nights we had lain as if in sleep till the hour of midnight had passed, and our ears and hearts had been pained, while we had listened for hours to the obscene jests, the horrid oaths, the dreadful blasphemies and filthy language of our guards, Colonel Price at their head, as they recounted to each other their deeds of rapine, murder, robbery, etc., which they had committed among the "Mormons" while at Far West and vicinity. They even boasted of defiling by force wives, daughters and virgins, and of shooting or dashing out the brains of men, women and children.

"I had listened till I became so disgusted, shocked, horrified, and so filled with the spirit of indignant justice that I could scarcely refrain from rising upon my feet and rebuking the guards; but had said nothing to Joseph, or any one else, although I lay next to him and knew he was awake. On a sudden he arose to his feet, and spoke in a voice of thunder, or as the roaring lion, uttering, as near as I can recollect, the following words:

"SILENCE, ye fiends of the infernal pit. In the name of Jesus Christ I rebuke you, and command you to be still; I will not live another minute and hear such language. Cease such talk, or you or I die THIS INSTANT!"

"He ceased to speak. He stood erect in terrible majesty. Chained, and without a weapon; calm, unruffled and dignified as an angel, he looked upon the quailing guards, whose weapons were lowered or dropped to the ground; whose knees smote together, and who, shrinking into a corner, or crouching at his feet, begged his pardon, and remained quiet till a change of guards.

"I have seen the ministers of justice, clothed in magisterial robes, and criminals arraigned before them, while life was suspended on a breath, in the Courts of England; I have witnessed a Congress in solemn session to give laws to nations; I have tried to conceive of kings, of royal courts, of thrones and crowns; and of emperors assembled to decide the fate of kingdoms;

but dignity and majesty have I seen but once, as it stood in chains, at midnight, in a dungeon in an obscure village of Missouri."

Autobiography of Parley P. Pratt, p. 210-11

The life of the prophet was filled with inspiring experiences. Although the world and Lucifer hated him and his work, yet many were moved to admire, and some admit to, the greatness of the man. The following article appeared shortly after Joseph Smith's martyrdom, printed in the Morning Chronicle, London, England, June 1851.

"Joseph Smith was indeed a remarkable man and in summing up his character it is extremely difficult to decide whether he were the vulgar imposter which it has been the fashion to consider him, or whether he were a sincere fanatic who believed what he taught. But whether an imposter who, for the purposes of his ambition, concocted the fraud of the Book of Mormon, or a fanatic who believed and promulgated a fraud originally concocted by some other person, it must be admitted, with no little zeal and courage, that his tact was great, that his talents for governing men were of no mean order, and that however glaring his deficiencies in early life may have been, he manifested as he grew older an ability both as an orator and as a writer, which showed that he possessed strong, natural gifts only requiring cultivation to have raised him to high reputation among better educated men.

"There are many incidents in his life which favor the supposition that he was guilty of a deliberate fraud in pretending to have revelations from heaven and in palming off upon the world his new Bible, but at the same time there is much in his later career which seems to prove that he really believed what he asserted, that he imagined himself to be in reality what he pretended, the chosen medium to convey a new Gospel to the world "The Inspired of Heaven," the Dreamer of Divine Dreams, and the companion of Angels.

"If he were an imposter, deliberately and coolly inventing and pertinaciously propagating a falsehood, there is much to be said; yet never was there an imposter more cruelly punished than he was, from the first moment of his appearance as a Prophet to the last. Joseph Smith, in consequence of his pretentions to be a seer and a Prophet of God, lived a life of continued misery and persecution. He was derided, assaulted and imprisoned; his life was one long scene of peril and distress, scarcely brightened by the brief beam of comparative repose which he enjoyed in his own city of Nauvoo.

"In the contempt showered upon his head his whole family shared; father, mother, wife, and friends were all alike involved in the ignominy of his pretentions and the sufferings that resulted. He lived for fourteen years amid vindictive enemies who never missed an opportunity to vilify, to harass, and to destroy him — and he died at last an untimely and miserable death involving in his fate a brother to whom he was tenderly attached.

"If anything can tend to encourage the supposition that Joseph Smith was a sincere enthusiast maddened with religious frenzies, as may have been before and will be afterwards, and that he had strong and invincible faith in his own pretentions and divine mission, it is the notability that unless supported by such feelings he would have renounced the unprofitable and ungrateful task and sought refuge from persecution and misery in private life and honorable industry. But whether sane or a lunatic, whether a liar or an honest man, it cannot be denied that he was one of the most extraordinary persons of his time, a man of rude genius who accomplished a greater work than he knew and whose name whatever he may have been whilst living will take its place among the notabilities of the world."

Like Peter, Paul, James, John, Stephen and others — though hated by the world — Joseph Smith loved people who loved the truth, and fearlessly carried out his assignment as did the apostles of old. He sealed his testimony as a martyr — a true witness to God's plan of salvation.

NEPHI

LEHI

JACOB
Son of Lehi

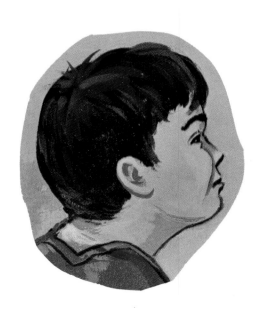

JOSEPH
Son of Lehi

18

Characters

Volume

JOSEPH OF EGYPT

JOSEPH SMITH

ISAIAH

LAMAN AND LEMUEL

MY father, Lehi, and I, Nephi, told my brothers what great things the Lord had done for them in bringing them out of Jerusalem. Then my father said how sorrowful he was that they had rebelled against the will of the Lord when we were crossing the sea. But God spared their lives, and they did not drown during the great storms. Lehi told them of the promised land that was now ours and of how blessed they were not to have been in Jerusalem when it was destroyed. We would have all perished had we remained! Despite the troubles of our long journey, we now had come to the promised land which was choice above all other lands. And it was to be a promised land to all who would come to it, for their inheritance, for none would come to it other than by the hand of the Lord!

See 2 Nephi 1:1-6

LEHI said that God had consecrated the land to everyone whom he should bring to it and that if everyone obeyed God's commandments it would be a land of liberty. If they were righteous, no one could bring its inhabitants into captivity. To keep the land from being overrun, God would keep it a secret from the nations for many years. It was, indeed, our land, and how blessed we would be if we could keep God's commandments!

But Lehi said that if the day should come when the people dwindle in unbelief after receiving God's blessings, the judgments of their Redeemer would come upon them. And these judgments would come even though they might know how the Lord created the earth, and all men, and what he did to make the earth such a marvellous place for his children. No matter how close the people might come to him, if they should fall into sin other nations would be given power over them, and they would be scattered and smitten.

See 2 Nephi 1:7-12

24

LEHI said, "My sons, awake from the deep sleep which is the sleep of hell, and shake off the chains that bind the children of men so that they are carried away captive down to the eternal gulf of misery and woe. Awake, for I will soon die and go into the glory of the Lord, who loves me. I want you to love him, and so be saved from the devil, who would carry you and your children down into the eternal pit. If you love the Lord and keep his commandments, you will prosper in the land. Arise from the dust, my sons, and let your father die in happiness. Do not rebel against your brother, Nephi, who has been steadfast in keeping the commandments and who has been an instrument of God in bringing us to this land. But I am afraid for you because you have accused him of seeking power and authority over you. He has sought the glory of God and your eternal welfare. What he has said and done is the Lord's will, even when he has shown you how sinful you were. My sons, listen to Nephi! Listen, sons of Ishmael! Listen Zoram, for you are a true friend to Nephi forever! Listen to Nephi, because you and all the generations that follow you will be blessed if you accept him as your leader and love him."

See 2 Nephi 1:13-32

" JACOB my son," Lehi said, "you were my firstborn in the wilderness. Your brothers have made you suffer, and your heart has been filled with sorrow. But you know the greatness of God and that he will turn your suffering to gain. Your soul will be blessed, you will live safely with Nephi, and you will serve the Lord. I know that you are redeemed, because of your Redeemer; for you have seen the fulness of time when the Lord will bring salvation to all men. When you were younger, you saw the Lord in his glory! You are as blessed as those to whom he will come. For you know that men have been cut off from him both spiritually and temporally and that it is only through him that they will be redeemed. So that the law will be satisfied, he will offer himself as a sacrifice for sin. Only through him can the dead be resurrected. Through him all mankind can be saved. All men will come unto God to be judged according to the truth and holiness in him. Whatever is opposite to him, his glory, and his joy will be punished."

See 2 Nephi 2:1-10

darkness

light

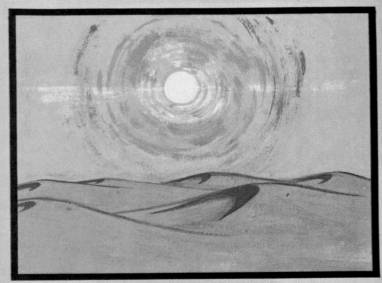

heat

cold

good

evil

"IF it were not for him, men would not be able to choose right from wrong, good from bad, holiness from misery. All things would be one, and a body would be as dead, having neither death, corruption nor incorruption, happiness nor misery, nor sense nor sensibility. If there were no opposites, there would be no choices to be made. He has made it possible for us to choose to be like him and so to be what we are, with the possibility of being saved. It is through him that we have purpose and meaning!

"Without him, it would be as if there were no day or night—and all things would remain the same, still, like a seed that could never grow, and nothing would change, and no beauty would exist, nor ugliness, nor joy, nor sorrow. It is our glory and eternal life to follow him!

"Without him, there is no purpose in creation, and this would be to destroy the wisdom of God and his eternal purposes, his power, his mercy, and his justice. If there is no law, there is no sin, and no righteousness. Without righteousness, there is no happiness; without righteousness and happiness, there is no punishment and misery; and without these things, there is no God. Without God, we do not exist, nor the earth, nor the creation of things to act and be acted upon—and all things must have vanished away."

See 2 Nephi 2:11–13

LEHI continued speaking to his sons: "God has created all things, both heaven and earth, and all things that are in them, even the forbidden fruit in opposition to the tree of life. Man must act for himself, for he is enticed one way or the other. An angel had fallen from heaven and became the devil because he sought evil. And so he became miserable forever. So he said to Eve in the Garden of Eden, 'Eat the forbidden fruit, and you shall not die, but you shall be as God, knowing good from evil.' When Adam and Eve ate the fruit, they were driven out of the garden. Then they and their children tilled the earth the rest of their days. The Lord caused them to live many years so that they would have a chance to repent; otherwise, they would be lost because of the sins of their parents. If Adam had not fallen, he would have remained in the garden, and there would have been no change, and no children, and in their innocence, Adam and Eve would have had no joy, for they knew no misery, and they could do no good, because they knew no sin. Adam fell that men might be; and men are, that they might have joy.

"The Messiah will come in the fulness of time, at the appointed time, to redeem all people from the fall. Then they will be free forever, knowing good from evil, and to act rather than being acted upon, except at the judgment of the Lord.

"Men are free on earth, and all things are given them which are for their good. They are free to choose liberty and eternal life or captivity and death. Eternal life is the life that the Lord offers to us. Satan wants us to choose death and be as miserable as he."

Lehi continued, "My sons, choose eternal life, and let the Lord help you by obeying his commandments. Do not choose the will of the flesh, through which the devil can capture you, for it will lead you into hell. I want only what is best for you—the everlasting welfare of your souls."

See 2 Nephi 2:14-21

"AND now, Joseph, the last of my children, you were born in the wilderness in the time of my afflictions. May the Lord bless this land for you, your brothers, and your children forever, so that you may be safe in it while you obey the Lord's commandments. May your seed never be completely destroyed, for I cherish you. I am a descendant of Joseph who was carried into Egypt and with whom the Lord made many covenants. That ancient Joseph saw what would happen to us, for we are the righteous branch of the house of Israel, even though we are broken off. But we will be remembered in the covenants of the Lord in the latter days, for the Messiah will be manifest to our descendants so that they will be brought out of darkness into light and out of captivity into freedom!"

See 2 Nephi 3:1-5

LEHI continued, "For Joseph testified that the Lord would raise up a choice seer among his children, who will tell them about the covenants that the Lord made with their fathers. He will be like Moses, who delivered his people from slavery. For he will convince them about the truth of the Lord's word. What he will write will confound false doctrines and bring peace. The Lord will bless him. 'Joseph' will be his name too, like his father's, and he will be like the first Joseph, for he will bring salvation to my people. He will be like Moses, who had power in a rod, but not in speech — but who had a spokesman to declare the truth."

See 2 Nephi 3:6-8; 12-15

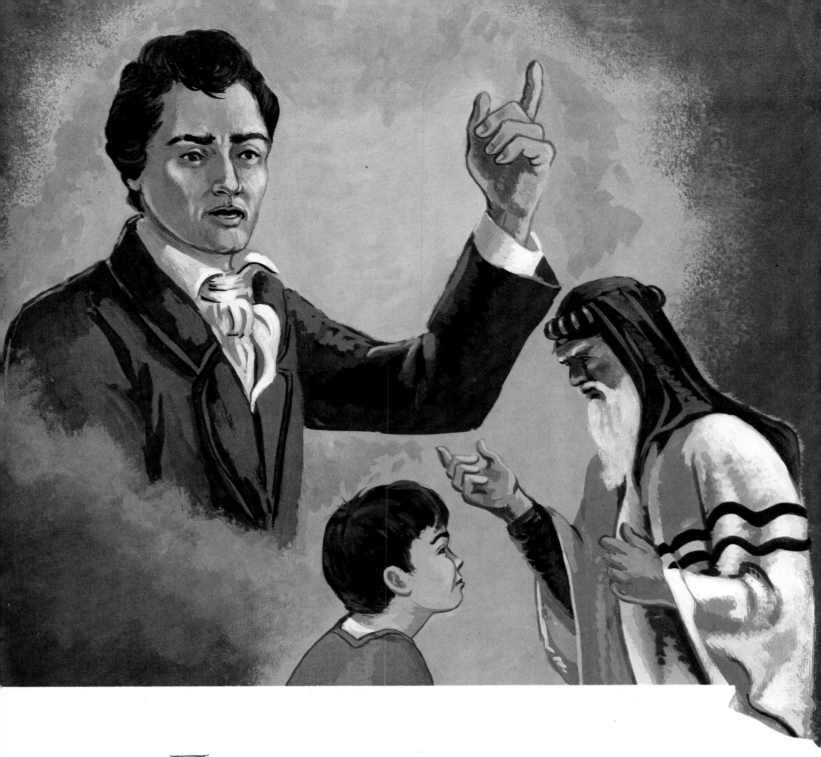

"YOUR children will possess this truth, but the Joseph of whom I speak will declare this truth as if your children were speaking from the dust. Your children will therefore cry repentance after many generations have passed away. The faith of this Joseph and his brethren in the Church of Jesus Christ in the latter days will be so strong that, although their words might be weak, they will convert your children to the truth of the Lord's covenants with your fathers. That is why you are blessed. So listen to your brother Nephi, who will lead and help you."

Lehi finished speaking. And now I, Nephi, want to speak about Joseph, who was carried into Egypt. He was a true prophet, and his prophecies are among the greatest we have. He prophesied about us and the generations that follow us. These prophecies are written on the plates of brass.

See 2 Nephi 3:18-25; 4:1-2

WHEN my father, Lehi, finished talking about the prophecies of Joseph, he called the children of Laman, his sons, and his daughters, and said to them: "The Lord has said that if you keep his commandments you will prosper in the land; but if you do not, you will be cut off from his presence. But I cannot die without blessing you. If you are brought up in the proper way, you will not fail. My blessing is that if you fail, the curse will be upon your parents for permitting evil to come into your lives. The Lord will not let you perish, but will be merciful to you."

Then Lehi called the sons and daughters of Lemuel, and said to them: "I give you the same blessing as I gave to the sons and daughters of Laman." And he gave the same blessing to the sons of Ishmael and his household.

Lehi then blessed Sam. He said that Sam's children would inherit the land as would my children, and that his children and mine would be one family, and that they would be blessed all their days.

See 2 Nephi 4:3-11

AFTER my father, Lehi, said all these things, he became very old. Then he died and was buried.

See 2 Nephi 4:12

38

NOT many days after Lehi died, Laman, Lemuel, and the sons of Ishmael became angry with me because the Lord reproved them and wanted them to be righteous.

See 2 Nephi 4:13

I, Nephi, knew that I should remind them about what the Lord wanted them to be and do. I had repeated what Lehi told them before he died. These things are written on my other plates, which contain more of a history. Upon the small plates I write the things of my soul, and many of the scriptures which are on the brass plates. I love the scriptures and think about them, and I write them so that my children will love them too.

See 2 Nephi 4:14-15

ALTHOUGH the Lord has been very good to me, I am weak and sad because of my little sins. I yield easily to temptation. When I want to sing the praises of the Lord, I remember my sins, and I groan. But I know the Lord, in whom I have faith. He has saved me in all my travels through the wilderness and on the sea. He so filled me with his love that my body was almost consumed. He has defeated my enemies, who quaked before me.

See 2 Nephi 4:17-35

Behold, he has heard me cry to him by day,
And he has revealed his truth to me in visions
That have come to me at night.
I have prayed mightily to him,
And my voice has risen to the heavens.
Angels have come down to me
And have ministered to me.
Upon the wings of the Spirit
My body has been carried away upon high mountains.
I have seen great things,
Too great for the eyes of men.
If I have seen so much glory,
If the Lord has been so kind to his children,
Why should I weep,
Why should my soul linger in the valley of sorrow,
Why should I waste away and grow weak
Because of my troubles and afflictions?

Why should I yield to sin?
Why should I yield to temptation,
And let the evil one have a place in my heart
And destroy my peace and afflict my soul?
Why should I let my enemy anger me?

Awake, my soul!
Do not sink in sin!
Rejoice, my heart,
And give no place to the enemy of my soul!
Do not become angry
And do not let me weaken in my afflictions.
Rejoice, O my heart,
And cry unto the Lord, and say:
"O Lord, I praise thee forever,
And my soul will rejoice in thee,
For thou art my God,
And the rock of my salvation.

"O Lord, wilt thou redeem my soul?
Wilt thou deliver me from my enemies?
Wilt thou let me shake even at the appearance of sin?

"May the gates of hell stay closed before me
Because my heart is broken
And my spirit is contrite!

"O Lord, do not shut the gates of righteousness before me,
That I may be humble in the path of the low valley,
That I may be strict in the plain road!

"O Lord, encircle me in the robe of thy righteousness!
Let me escape from my enemies!
Make my path straight before me!
Do not let me stumble,
But clear the way before me.

"O Lord, I have trusted thee,
And I will trust thee, forever.
I will not trust the arm of flesh,
For he who does is cursed,
Nor will I put my trust in man,
Or make flesh my arm.

"I know that my God gives liberally to him who asks,
And if I honor him, he will give me
What I ask in righteousness.

"Therefore, O God, I cry unto thee,
Who art the rock of my righteousness.
My voice will always ascend unto thee,
My rock and my everlasting God.
Amen." *

See 2 Nephi 4:17-35

*The poetic form is an adaptation by Dr. Clinton F. Larson of the poetic
nature of the scripture from which it came.

I, Nephi, cried to the Lord because my brothers were angry. They were so angry that they tried to kill me. Again they said that I was trying to rule over them. They said that if they killed me my words would no longer cause them trouble. Then I would not be their ruler, for they said ruling over our family was their right. But the Lord warned me to leave them and flee into the wilderness with those who would go with me. I took my family, Zoram and his family, Sam, my older brother and his family, Jacob and Joseph, my sisters, and others. They believed in the Lord's warnings and in the revelations of God, and listened to me.

See 2 Nephi 5:1-6

WE took our tents and other things that were possible to take on our journey. We travelled for many days and then pitched our tents. We called the place Nephi, and we called ourselves the people of Nephi, or the Nephites. We kept all the commandments of the Lord, according to the law of Moses.

The Lord was with us! We prospered in the land. We sowed seeds, and we reaped abundant harvests. We raised flocks, and herds, and many different animals.

I, Nephi, had brought the brass plates and the ball, or compass, which the Lord prepared for my father, Lehi.

Not only did we prosper, but our numbers increased too.

See 2 Nephi 5:7-13

I took the sword of Laban and made many swords like it. I wanted to be sure that we could defend ourselves against the Lamanites if they attacked us.

See 2 Nephi 5:14

I, Nephi, began to teach my people to build buildings. Part of this teaching included how to work wood, iron, copper, brass, steel, gold, silver, and precious ores, to put them to good use.

Then I built a temple like the temple of Solomon, although it did not contain so many precious things. We did not have many things that we might have gotten if we were in Jerusalem. But we were nevertheless proud of our temple because our best efforts went into it, and the workmanship was very fine.

See 2 Nephi 5:15-17

ONE day the people came to me and asked me to be their king. We had worked hard to build a fine community, and they felt that they needed a strong government. I, Nephi, did not want them to have a king, but I wanted to work for them as hard as I could. The words of the Lord had been fulfilled that I should be the ruler and teacher of my brothers until they sought to kill me.

See 2 Nephi 5:18-19

THE Lord had said that if my brothers and their families would not listen to me they would be cut off. The Lord caused a curse to come upon them because they were so sinful. They had so hardened their hearts against the Lord that their hearts were like flint. Because the Lord did not want them to be enticing to my people, he caused their skin to turn dark.

The Lord said, "If they do not repent, I shall cause them to be loathsome to the Nephites. If they marry any of the Nephites, the children will also be cursed

in the same way." The Lord said these things, and they were done! These people became idle people, full of mischief and trickery. Rather than building communities, they became only hunters of beasts of prey.

The Lord said to me: "They shall be the enemy of your descendants. If your descendants do not remember me and obey my commandments, the descendants of your brothers will destroy them."

See 2 Nephi 5:20-25

To help my people love the Lord and follow his commandments, I consecrated Jacob and Joseph as priests and teachers over the land of my people. We became a very happy people.

See 2 Nephi 5:26

IT had been thirty years since we left Jerusalem, and I, Nephi, had kept the record of my people since that time. The Lord said to me: "Make other plates and write on them whatever is fine and good for your people." I obeyed, and I knew that my work would please my people if they loved the Lord. If they wanted to know more about their history, they could search through my other plates.

When forty years had passed away, we already had had wars with the Lamanites.

See 2 Nephi 5:28-34

JACOB said to my people: "I have been called of God and ordained after his holy order, and my brother Nephi, whom you look upon as your king or protector, has consecrated me. I have told you many things about the Lord and his work. Now I want to tell you about the future. Nephi wants me to read to you from the words of Isaiah—the part about your being like the house of Israel.

"The Lord God has said, 'The Gentiles will bring the standard of God to the people, and they will help your sons and daughters. Kings and queens will be like parents to them.'

"The Lord has shown me that those whom we left behind at Jerusalem have been slain or carried away as captives. But they will return! The Lord will show himself to them, but they will torture him and crucify him!

"Then his judgment will come upon them, and they shall be smitten and afflicted. They will be driven to and fro, but the prayers of the faithful will keep them from perishing. They will be scattered, punished, and hated, but the Lord will be merciful. When they know that the Lord is their Redeemer, they will be gathered to the land of their inheritance.

"If the Gentiles do not fight against Zion, they shall be saved.

"The Lord will come again and save his people. He will come in great glory and destroy their enemies through fire, tempest, earthquakes, bloodshed, pestilence, and famine, and they shall know that the Lord is God, the Holy One of Israel. The captives of the mighty shall be set free; the Lord will deliver his covenant people. All people will know that the Lord is the Savior and Redeemer."

See 2 Nephi 6:1-18

JACOB continued preaching to my people. "Yes, the Lord has said through
Isaiah that he would not abandon his people. When he and they are separated,
it is because the people have been wicked. 'My people, do not think that I do not
have the power to save you. I could dry up the sea and make the floor of the sea a
wilderness where the fish would die and rot. I could clothe the heavens with blackness. But I speak wisdom and encouragement to the house of Israel. I will suffer

for you, if need be. But the Lord God will help me, and I shall not be ashamed. He will justify me and pronounce me without guilt and make me strong. Then who can stand against me? Those who do will be as an old garment that is ready to be thrown away. Who, then, among you fears God, obeys his servant, and walks in darkness without light? Repent, and accept the salvation that I offer you.'"

See 2 Nephi 7:1-11

"THE Lord has said, 'Listen to me and seek righteousness. Remember Abraham and Sarah, who are the father and mother of Israel. Remember that I called Abraham and blessed him. I will make Zion a garden of the Lord, instead of a desert; it will be a place of music and thanksgiving. For the law shall come from me, and my judgment will be glorious and happy for those who obey it. The lands and islands of the earth await my judgment.

"'Though the heavens and earth may vanish, the salvation that I offer you will last forever. Do not fear men or what they may say. Awake and be strong, O arm of the Lord, for you have cut Rahab, which is Egypt, and have wounded the dragon, which is the pharaoh. You divided the sea and made it possible for my people to pass over it unharmed. The redeemed of the Lord will return singing to Zion, and my peace, holiness, and joy will be with them. Do not forget me, for though I made the heavens and earth I love you and worry about what your enemies may do to you. You are in the shadow of my hand, and I want you to know that you are my people.'"

See 2 Nephi 8:1-16

"STAND up, O Jerusalem! Your sons have fainted—all but two, and they, my prophets, are full of the fury of my rebuke that you are sinful. But I will turn my fury away from you upon your enemies, who have enslaved you. Be strong, Zion! Put on your beautiful garments, O Jerusalem! Shake the dust away from you, and in your glory accept eternal life.'"

See 2 Nephi 8:17-25

JACOB continued: "My brethren, now I want to tell you about the covenants of the Lord with the house of Israel down through history, until the time they will be restored to the true church and will be gathered to the land of their inheritance. The Lord will appear in Jerusalem, from whence we came. He will be subject to men and die for all men so that they will become subject to him. Adam and Eve disobeyed God, and so they fell and were cut off from the Lord. Because they became subject to death, they needed to be resurrected and receive the benefits of infinite atonement. Otherwise, the devil would rule them forever, and they would become like him and be guilty of murder and secret works of darkness. But men can escape like him and be guilty of murder and secret works of darkness. But men can escape from him — and the death of the body and spirit! The Holy One of Israel will make death only temporary, and the grave shall deliver its dead. And the spiritual death, which is hell, will also give up its dead! This is the power of the resurrection of the Savior. All men will become incorruptible, and they will become immortal, having perfect knowledge. And they will all come before the judgment seat of the Holy One of Israel and face the justice of God. They will be seen for what they are; the righteous will remain righteous and the devil and his followers will go away into everlasting fire. The righteous will receive eternal joy.

"They who believe in the Holy One of Israel and who endure the crosses of the world will in joy inherit the kingdom of God forever. He will suffer the pains of every descendant of Adam in order that all might be resurrected. He commands them all to repent, and be baptized in his name, and have perfect faith in him to be saved in the kingdom of God. Those who do not repent will be condemned. He has given a law. Without law, there is no punishment; without punishment, there is no condemnation; without condemnation, his mercies have claim on them because of the atonement and they are delivered by his power.

"The atonement fulfilled justice for those who do not have the law; so that they are saved from death and hell and the devil, and the lake of fire and brimstone, which is endless torment. They are restored to God, who gave them breath, which is the Holy One of Israel. But if someone has received the law and the commandments of God, and ignores them, how awful will be his condition! Many who think that they are learned and wise have put God's commandments aside. They will perish in their error. Learning is good only when men listen to God. God is the salvation of all men, and they must obey him if they are not to be swept away. It is a terrible thing to transgress against God!

"Being carnally-minded is death; being spiritually-minded is eternal life. All men will be judged according to their works — so, my brethren, shake iniquity from your souls! Prepare yourselves now for the judgment of the Holy One of Israel! You know that we have been sinful, and that is why I speak to you as I do. Accept the Lord in your hearts and pray to him continually. I, Jacob, will stop for now, but tomorrow let me continue telling you about the Lord and his ways. Amen.".

See 2 Nephi 9:1-54

"NOW I, Jacob, want to talk to you, my beloved brethren, about the righteous branch of Israel. The promises we have received have to do with the flesh. Many of our children will perish in the flesh for their unbelief, but God will be merciful to many, and our children will be restored so that they may learn the true knowledge of their Redeemer. Christ will come among the Jews in a very wicked part of the world, and he will be crucified. The Jews will either be destroyed or scattered after that time.

See 2 Nephi 10:1-6

"BUT someday they will return. For the Lord has said, 'When the Jews believe in me, that I am the Christ, then according to my covenant with their fathers, I shall restore them to the lands of their inheritance from their dispersion, from the isles of the sea and from the four parts of the earth. The nations of the Gentiles will be great in my eyes, and will help them gather.' Kings and queens will act as their foster parents. The promises of the Lord to the Gentiles are great, and this is a truth that cannot be disputed."

See 2 Nephi 10:7-9

"AND the Lord says: 'This land shall be a land of your inheritance, and the Gentiles shall be blessed upon it. It shall be a land of liberty, and no kings will rule it. It will be protected from all other nations, and whoever fights against it will perish. If anyone raises up a king, he will also perish, for I am the king of this land, and I will be a light to those who obey me. That my covenants may be fulfilled, I will destroy the secret works of darkness, of murders, and of abomina-

tions. My beloved brethren, I will afflict your descendants by the hand of the Gentiles and number the Gentiles among the house of Israel. I consecrate this choice land to you and your children as the land of your inheritance!' So my brethren, I, Jacob, beg of you to remember our merciful God by sinning no more, for he has brought us here to the promised land."

See 2 Nephi 10:10-20

"THE promises of the Lord are great to our brethren who live on the islands of the sea. Yes, they too were led away from Israel by the hand of God, and they too will be remembered. Cheer up, my brethren, and remember that you are free to act for yourselves — free to choose the way to everlasting death or the way to eternal life. Love the Lord, for it is only through him that you are saved. May God raise you from death by the power of the resurrection and from everlasting death by the power of the atonement, that you may return to him."

See 2 Nephi 10:21-25

70

AND now I, Nephi, recall that Jacob said many more things to my people, but I have caused only this much to be written down. Now I want to write more of the words of Isaiah, for they fill me with joy. I want all my children to have these words because he saw the Redeemer, as Jacob and I have seen him. The words of all three prove that my words are true. And even more witnesses will come to prove that the words of God are true. The Christ will come! Everything God has given to men points to his coming! If there is no Christ, there is no God, and if there is no God then we do not exist. But he will come in his own time. And now for the words of Isaiah!

See 2 Nephi 11:1-8

THIS is the word that Isaiah, the son of Amos, saw about Judah and Jerusalem. "In the last days the word of God will be fulfilled when the mountain of the Lord's house shall be established in the top of the mountains, and shall be exalted above the hills, and all nations shall flow unto it. And many people shall go and say, 'Come, and let us go up to the mountain of the Lord, to the house of the God of Jacob; and he will teach us of his ways, and we will walk in his paths; for out

of Zion shall go forth the law, and the word of the Lord from Jerusalem.' The Lord will judge among the ways of nations and will rebuke many people for their wrongdoing. Then these people will turn their weapons of destruction into machines that will serve the peace. Nations will not wage war any more, and they will not be interested even in learning about it."

See 2 Nephi 12:1-4

"COME, O house of Jacob, and walk in the light of the Lord. Do not listen to false friends and to those who would lead you astray. They may have great wealth and may possess many things that they say are desirable, but they are not of me. Do not covet possessions of men, for the Lord in his majesty will punish you if you do. And the Lord will humble those who are filled with pride about themselves and their accomplishments and who try to lead his children astray."

74   See 2 Nephi 12:5-11

"THE Lord has said, 'The meek shall rule the mighty, for this is my judgment. Wo to Jerusalem, and Judah, for they have sinned and have provoked me. All my people shall receive the judgment they deserve. They will be judged according to their heritage, that they have received from their fathers. Some have thrown their blessings away, and some have been deprived of them. But whoever is guilty, even those who are vain, will be judged for what they are. It does not matter how richly they are clothed, or how many tinkling ornaments they have, or how fancy and rich they have become — the Lord sees them for what they are, and all that they think they are and all that they possess will become bitter and foul to them.'"

See 2 Nephi 13:1-26

IN the day of the Lord's judgment, the latter days, righteous women will seek out righteous men and take their names to avoid reproach. For in that day the branch of the Lord will be beautiful and glorious. Those who are left in Zion and who remain in Jerusalem shall be called holy, for the Lord shall have cleansed them with the spirit of judgment and the spirit of burning. To protect them, the Lord will give them a cloud and smoke by day and a shining flame by night, which will be seen as the glory of Zion."

See 2 Nephi 14:1-6

ISAIAH continued: "The Lord has given his children the bountiful earth, and he has done all he could to help them. If they do not obey him, he will ruin or destroy their harvests, and their great cities will decay and will be abandoned. The captivity of my people will be their bad habits and behavior, for they will have no knowledge of the Lord. And there will be no honorable men to help them. The gates of hell will open up before them, and they will slip through if they rejoice in sin. Wo be to them who are not honest and true! Wo be to them who despise the Holy One of Israel! For he will lift up an ensign to the nations, and all will recognize him in his power. Then he will come to judge the world — all that men are, and all that they have created — and the righteous will be blessed."

See 2 Nephi 15:1-30

"IN the year that King Uzziah died, I, Isaiah, saw the Lord sitting on a throne in his temple. And the heavenly host cried, 'Holy, holy, holy is the Lord of Hosts; the earth is full of his glory.' And I felt guilty because I, in my sins, had seen the Lord. Then an angel flew to me and put a hot coal against my mouth! He said, 'This has touched my lips. Your iniquity is taken away!' Then a voice said, 'Whom shall I send?' And I said, 'Here am I; send me!' It said, 'Go and tell this people that they hear and see the truth but do not understand it. Tell them that they forsake the Lord. Only a few will return to the Lord, to understand him and love him.'"

See 2 Nephi 16:1-13

"AND it came to pass in the days of Ahaz that Syria was in league with the northern tribes of Israel under Ephraim. The Lord said to me, Isaiah, that I should meet Ahaz and tell him not to fear Syria and Ephraim, although they threatened to go to war against the southern kingdom for not helping them oppose the Assyrians. The threat would not be carried out! Syria and the northern tribes would fall before the Assyrians. The Lord afterwards spoke to Ahaz: 'Ask a sign of the Lord.' But Ahaz said, 'I will not tempt the Lord.' Then the Lord said: 'A virgin shall bear a son, and call him Immanuel.' He will choose the good always. If you and your people do not choose the good and avoid evil alliances, you will suffer and your lands will be laid waste. And this will be true for those who rule after you and the people whom they rule."

See 2 Nephi 17:1-25

" I , the prophet Isaiah, called two witnesses, Uriah the priest and Zechariah the son of Jeberechiah, and I went to the prophetess, who bore a son. After his birth, this son would not learn to call to his father and mother by their names before Assyria would destroy Syria and Ephraim, so near is that destruction. The tribes of Ephraim will be taken north and will disappear, and nothing they do can prevent this from happening. The Lord could have helped them if they had listened to him. But they do not speak the word of God, and there is not light in them; therefore trouble and darkness and anguish are to be with them."

See 2 Nephi 18:1-22

"BUT the troubles of the people shall not be as great as some other tribes of Israel, as for example, those people who shall be afflicted near the Red Sea. The people that walked in darkness have seen the light. There is promise! For unto us a son is born, and the government shall be upon his shoulders; and his name shall be called, Wonderful, Counselor, The Mighty God, The Everlasting Father, The Prince of Peace. There is no end to the growth of his government, upon the throne of David and everywhere, and justice will reign forever! But now the Lord will punish his people who do not call unto him, even with this great promise of their salvation. Assyria will be the rod of his judgment. But a few will escape from the anger of Assyria and will return to their homeland, and then Assyria will suffer for its pride, its lack of spiritual values."

See 2 Nephi 19 and 20

ABRAHAM

JUDAH

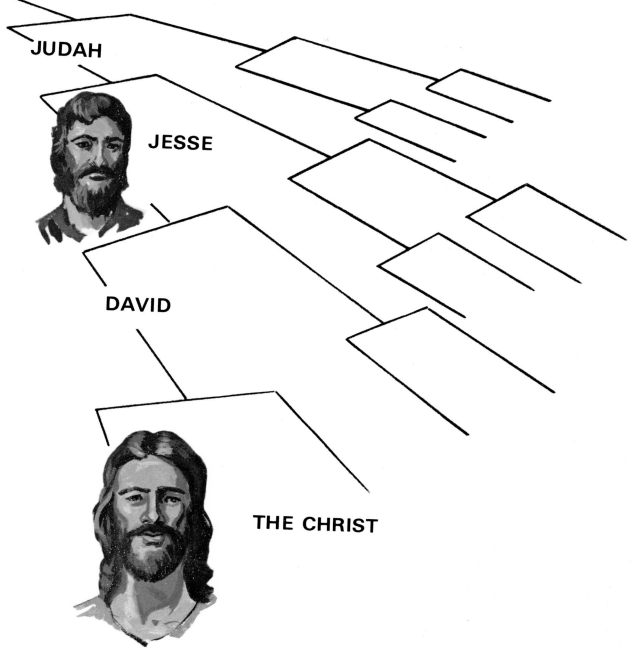

JESSE

DAVID

THE CHRIST

"AND there shall come forth a rod out of the stem of Jesse, who shall be called the Christ. The Spirit of the Lord shall be with him, the spirit of understanding the power of truth. He will help the humble and the poor and will fight against wickedness. Faith will be his standard."

See 2 Nephi 21:1-5

"THEN a wonderful time will come when it will be possible for the lamb and and the wolf and all other natural enemies to live together peacefully, and a little child shall lead them! This will happen because the earth will be full of the knowledge of the Lord."

See 2 Nephi 21:6-9

"IN that time the Lord shall set his hand again the second time to recover the remnant of his people which shall be left. Then he shall set up an ensign to all nations and gather the children of Israel and Judah to him from the four corners of the earth. And Ephraim and Judah will not vex each other. The children of Israel will come to him over a great highway that he will prepare for them. And all his people will sing to him and praise him and call him the Holy One of Israel.

"Those who fight against the Lord will be destroyed, and Babylon will fall as did Sodom and Gomorrah. But the children of Israel will dwell in happiness in the house of the Lord and in the lands of their promise."

See 2 Nephi 21:10-16; 22; 23; 24:1-11

"THE king of Babylon will journey to hell, where his power will be broken. He will see the wicked rulers of the world there, in their sorrow and weakness. His pride and pomp will be brought down to the grave."

"He will be like Satan, the miserable and fallen angel, because he wanted to be like the Most High God. And Assyria will be thrown down and trodden upon. No one should rejoice over the troubles of Israel, because they will not last as will those of Palestina. The Lord will not let the wicked reign unpunished; therefore, the wicked should grieve to know what awaits them."

See 2 Nephi 24:9-11

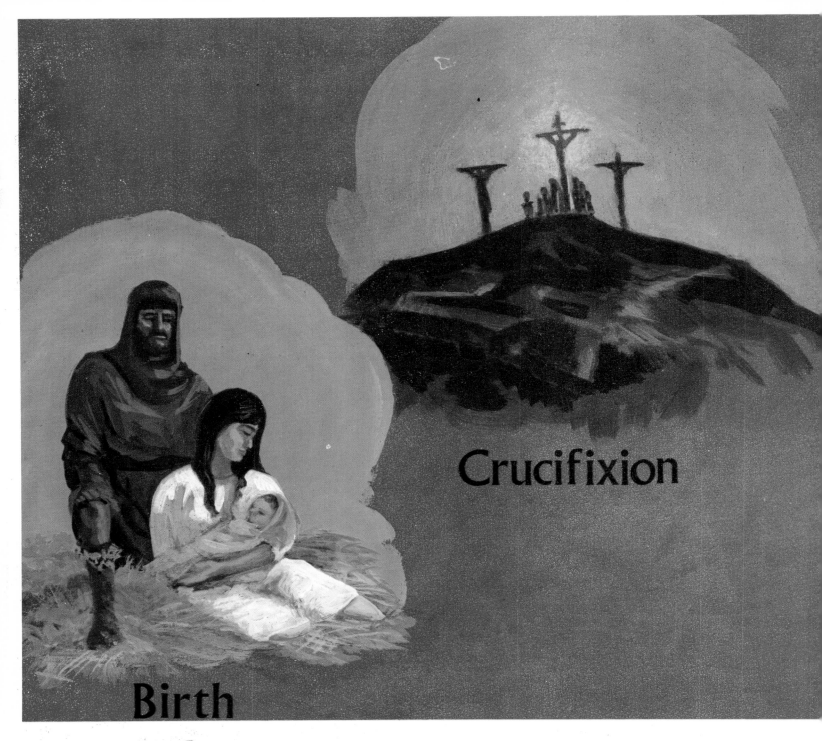

Crucifixion

Birth

NOW I, Nephi, declare to my people that though the words of Isaiah may be hard for them to understand they are nevertheless in the true spirit of prophecy. All those who are filled with that spirit will find them plain and easy, and I testify that this kind of plainness is dear to me. I delight in the words of Isaiah. And I know they will come to pass.

The Jews understand them. And I, Nephi, understand them, even those things close to the Jews, because of my experiences as a boy in their land.

But now I want to continue with my prophecies, which are according to my plainness, and I know that they will be understood by my people and by the Saints of the latter days, to whom they will be of great value.

Jesus the Christ will someday come among the Jews, and they will reject him and crucify him. He will be laid in a sepulchre, and after three days he will rise from the dead, with healing in his wings. All those who believe on his name will be saved in the kingdom of God. Then Jerusalem will be destroyed again because of those who do not believe. Then the Jews will be scattered among the nations. After many generations the Jews will be persuaded to believe in him and his atonement, which is infinite for mankind. Then the Lord will do a marvellous work and a wonder among the children of men. His children will be gathered!

Resurrection

Appearance To Nephites

My brethren, I have spoken plainly so that you cannot mistake me. I write these things so that salvation can be ours and so that the descendants of Joseph will never perish as long as the earth should stand. And the nations will be judged by what the Lord has revealed for their benefit. For we know that it is by his grace that men are saved. Listen, my people, and change your ways. Believe in Christ, and do not deny him.

After the Christ is risen, he will show himself to you. But he will come after the wicked have brought destruction on themselves and their lands and cities. O the pain and the anguish of my soul for the loss of the slain of my people! But I say that the ways of God are just.

The just, though they may be persecuted, will look forward to Christ and will not perish. For he will appear to them! When almost four generations have passed away in the peace that he will bring them, then my people will fall into sin and will choose the devil. They will sell themselves for nothing, and destruction will come upon them quickly. The spirit of the Lord will not always strive with man, and without it he will fail.

It is necessary that the Jews and the Gentiles be convinced that Jesus is the Christ, the Eternal God. Men will be saved according to their faith in him.

See 2 Nephi 24:12-32; 25; 26:1-13

I, Nephi, prophesy to you about the last days, when God shall bring these things to pass. After my descendants and those of my brethren have dwindled in unbelief, and the Lord has brought them low, into the dust, and they are not, yet the prayers of the righteous will still be heard. Our descendants will not be forgotten! They will speak out of the ground, from the dust! Their voice will be as one that has a familiar spirit. The Lord will give him power that he may whisper about them.

See 2 Nephi 26:14-18

90

THEN those who have dwindled in unbelief shall be smitten by the hand of the Gentiles.

See 2 Nephi 26:19

BUT in the last days, which are the days of the Gentiles, the nations will become very wicked. Then the Lord will come again, with great storms upon the earth and sea and with a devouring fire. All the nations that fight against Zion will be like a bad dream. They will not be able to satisfy their desires and will lose control of their destinies. It will seem as if they have lost their leaders.

See 2 Nephi 27:1-5

THE Lord will bring forth a book from the dead which will make it seem as if they have slumbered. It will be sealed. In it will be a revelation from God about the whole history of the world, from beginning to end. The book will be delivered to a man who will deliver the words of the book to another. But he will not deliver the words of the sealed book, for it was sealed by the power of God. And the revelation that was sealed will be kept until the Lord's own due time.

See 2 Nephi 27:6-10

THE day will come when the words of the book will be broadcast from tall buildings by the power of Christ, and all things shall be revealed to men that have ever been among them and that ever will be, to the end of the earth.

See 2 Nephi 27:11

WHEN the book shall be delivered to the man, about whom I have spoken, it shall be hidden from the world, except to three witnesses. They will see it by the power of God, and they will testify to the truth of the book and to the things it contains.

See 2 Nephi 27:12

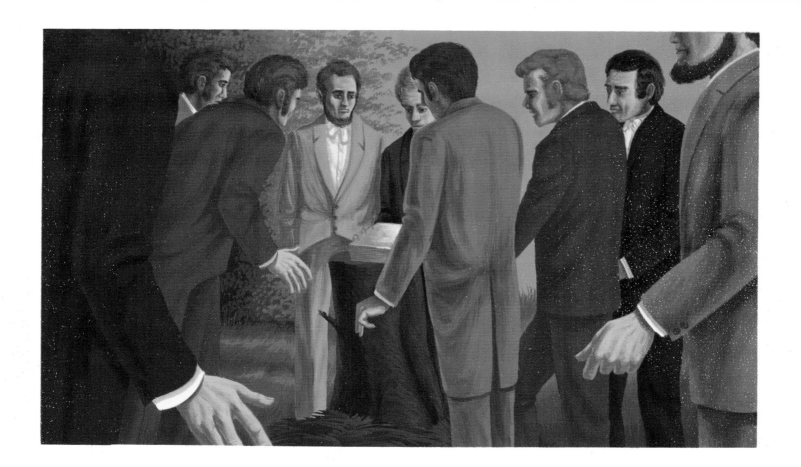

AND no other will see it, except a few, according to the will of God, and they will bear testimony of his word to men. The Lord has said that the words of the faithful should speak as if from the dead, and he will choose as many witnesses as he will need to establish his word.

See 2 Nephi 27:13-14

THEN the Lord will say to him to whom he shall deliver the book: Take these words that are not sealed, deliver them to another, that he may show them to a learned man, and say: Read this, please. And the learned man shall say: Bring it and I will. But his purpose will be to get money, not for the glory of God. The man will say: I cannot bring the book, for it is sealed. Then the learned will say: I cannot read it.

See 2 Nephi 27:15-18

THE learned man will not be able to read the book because he will reject it in his heart, but the unlearned man will be able to read it because he will accept it as the truth and will cherish it. But the Lord will tell him: Do not touch the sealed part of the book, for I will bring it forth in my own due time. He will read what the Lord wants him to read, and then he will seal it up and hide it unto the Lord. For the Lord blesses men according to their faith. The Lord shall say: I will do a marvellous work and a wonder among this people, for the wisdom of their wise and learned men shall perish.

See 2 Nephi 27:19-27

THE Lord will bless his children. The Lord will give them spiritual understanding. The deaf will hear the words of the book, the blind will see, and everyone will rejoice in him. It is then, only a little while until Lebanon will be turned into a fruitful field, like a forest. The Lord's enemies, who deny the truth of the book, will be defeated.

See 2 Nephi 27:28-35

I, Nephi, testify that these things will come to pass. What is written out of the book shall be of great value, especially to our descendants, who are a remnant of the house of Israel. The day will come when the false churches will say that they are of the Lord. These churches will contend with each other; they will teach what they have learned, but they will deny the Holy Ghost; and they will say that the Holy One of Israel has finished his work! They will say that he is not a God of miracles! So they will say: Eat, drink, and be merry, for tomorrow we die. Nevertheless, they will say, fear God—he will justify committing a little sin. He will then punish us a little after we die, but he will save us in the kingdom of God.

Moreover, some will teach vain and foolish doctrines and be proud of themselves for so doing, and they will try to hide their work from the Lord. But the blood of the saints shall cry from the ground against them.

They will rob the poor and persecute the meek. They will be proud and wicked, and all will go astray but a few of the humble followers of Christ who do not follow the precepts of men.

The wicked will be thrust down into hell and perish. But even so, whoever repents will be saved.

See 2 Nephi 28:1-17

THE devil will have great power in that day, and he will stir people up to such a rage in their hearts against what is good that they will surely perish. Others will fall into a false security and say: All is well in Zion. But the devil will drag them down to hell. To still others he will say: There is no hell, for I am the devil and I would tell you if there were. In this way he chains them and keeps them forever. Wo to him who says that all is well in Zion and denies the Holy Ghost! Wo to him who says that he no longer needs the word of God.

But the Lord will inspire those who follow his precepts to gain wisdom, and they will be blessed beyond their greatest expectations, no matter how humble they may be.

See 2 Nephi 28:18-32

I, Nephi, know that there will be many among whom the Lord will do a marvel-lous work. The Lord will set his hand a second time to recover his people, and it will be through me and my descendants that his words will come! But many of the Gentiles will say: A Bible! A Bible! We have got a Bible. We have got a Bible, and there cannot be any more Bible. But the Bible will come from the Jews, whom many of the Gentiles will despise! The Lord loves his ancient covenant people, the Jews, among whom he has worked and will work so diligently. Many of the Gentiles will not help the Jews, but they will accept and use the scriptures that he has given and will give to them! The Lord will always remember his people and try to save them.

The Lord will give his word to all the nations of the earth, and he will even remember his people on the islands of the sea! He sorrows that men cannot accept his word as he in his love gives it. He delights in the testimony of one, of two, of a family, and of a nation, according to their own faith. He gives the gospel to each and to many because he wants to show them that he is the same Lord always. He will speak wherever he will and whenever he will, according to his own pleasure.

See 2 Nephi 29:1-10

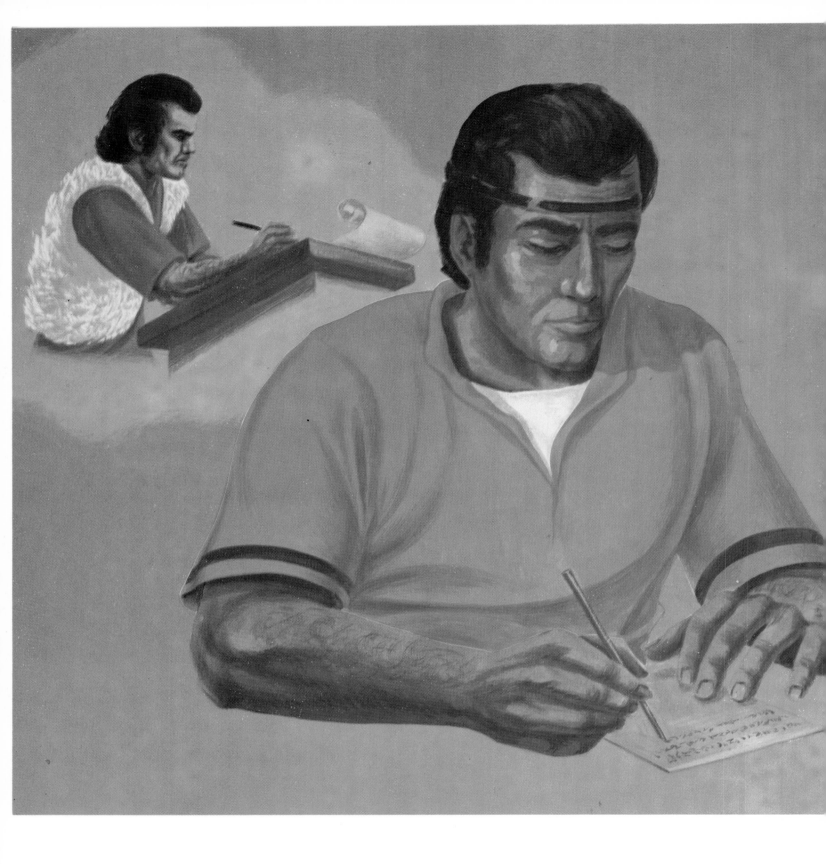

THE Lord commands that all men shall write the words that he gives them, for out of the books in which they appear the Lord will judge the world, according to the works of every man. He will speak to the Jews, the Nephites, and the other tribes of Israel, and to all the nations of the earth! Then the tribes and the nations will exchange their records of the gospel, for their salvation. The word of the Lord will be gathered in one!

See 2 Nephi 29:11-14

MY brethren, you should not suppose that you are more righteous than the Gentiles shall be. Keeping the commandments of God will save us all. The Gentiles who repent are the covenant people of the Lord, and the Jews who do not will be cast off. The book that will be written to the Gentiles will convert many, and they will bring it to our descendants. Then they will learn that we came out of Jerusalem and that they are descendants of the Jews. The gospel of Jesus Christ will be preached to them, and they will learn about their fathers and about the Lord's ministry among their fathers. They will become very happy, for they will know that it is the Lord who blesses them. The scales of darkness will fall away from their eyes, and they will become a fair and delightsome people.

See 2 Nephi 30:1-6

I, Nephi, prophesy that in that day the Jews that are scattered will also believe in Christ. They will gather. The Lord will begin his work of restoring his people, and in righteousness he will judge the poor and meek, and give them their just heritage.

See 2 Nephi 30:7-9

THE Lord will cause a great division among the peoples of the earth. He will destroy the wicked, but he will spare his people. His people will follow him, support him, and help him bring to pass the immortality and eternal life of man.

See 2 Nephi 30:10-11

AND then the thousand years of peace—the millennium—will come. The wolf and the lamb, the leopard and the calf, and the young lion and the fatling will live side by side in peaceful innocence, and a little child will lead them. Satan will be bound, and he will be kept utterly from doing harm. The work of the Lord will be fulfilled, and all things given to men will be revealed.

See 2 Nephi 30:12

I, Nephi, testify that the Lord will speak to you in your understanding when you obey his commandments.

I have spoken to you about the prophet who will baptize the Lord. If the Lord needs baptism, then we, who are not holy, need it much, much more than he! He humbled himself in his purity and innocence, before the Father, to be obedient to him. Then, as he is baptized, the Holy Ghost will descend upon him in the form of a dove. The Lord by this means shows the straight and narrow way that we should follow. The Father wants us to repent and be baptized in the name of his Beloved Son. Those who do will receive the gift of the Holy Ghost. Then you will also receive spiritual gifts without measure. You will speak with the tongue of angels and shout praises to the Holy One of Israel. If, then, you should deny him, it would be better that you had never known him. The words of Jesus Christ are true and faithful. So to receive eternal blessings you must keep them, honor them, and live according to them throughout your whole life. You must endure to the end.

This is the only way you can be saved. And this is why I, Nephi, have been telling you about the past and the future, and about the ways of the Lord. Repent and be baptized. Then the remission of your sins will come by fire and by the Holy Ghost.

Have you done as I have asked you to do? No. You have come as far as you have only by the grace of Christ and his merit. Be steadfast. Possess the perfect brightness of hope. Work for your salvation. If you endure to the end, you shall have eternal life. There is no other way. My brethren, this is my testimony of the true doctrine of Christ.

What will you do when you follow this way? Why do you worry? You will speak with angels by the power of the Holy Ghost! Your progress will be beautiful and great, and you will have a marvellous spirit of peace, which will be a joy to you, beyond your imagination to conceive of it. The Lord will lead you.

And now I, Nephi, cannot say more. The Spirit has stopped me, and I am left to mourn because of the evil practices of men. They will not listen!

If you listen to the Spirit, you will pray. Pray always, and do all things in the name of the Lord. Then what you do will be consecrated to you and the Lord, for the welfare of your soul.

See 2 Nephi 31:1-21; 32:1-9

111

OW I, Nephi, cannot write in an effective, powerful way. When a man speaks, the Holy Ghost can reach the hearts of his listeners. But because men harden their hearts, they do not put great value upon writing. But I have written what I have written, and I know my writing is of great value to my people. For I pray continually for my people, by day, and I weep for them at night. I cry to my God in faith, and I know he will hear me.

The Lord will accept and consecrate my prayers for my people, and my weak written words will be made strong for them. My words will reach the hearts of my people and will persuade them to do good. They will learn of their fathers. They will learn of Jesus and believe in him. They will endure to the end, which is life eternal.

Those who oppose my words are of the devil, for I speak plainly about the truth. I love all men. I love the Jews from whom I came. I have charity for the Gentiles, who are not saved except they love the Lord and obey him through the day of probation.

My beloved brethren, and also the Jew, and everyone to the ends of the earth, believe what I say. I give you the words of the Lord. Believe in them and believe in Christ. He gave them to me, and they teach all men to do good.

The Lord will show you that these words are true when he faces you at the judgment seat and judges you. You will know that I have been commanded to write them, despite my weakness and my lack of ability.

I pray that some of us, if not all, will be saved in the kingdom of heaven when the world shall come to an end. Now, Israel, and all people to the ends of the earth, I speak as a voice crying from the dust: Farewell until the day of judgment comes! Remember me! Remember the Lord! Amen.

See 2 Nephi 33:1-14

Pearls for Thought

by Joseph N. Revill

There are few places in scripture that carry a better example of the fulfillment of the Lord's word, as spoken by one of his prophets, than in the Second Book of Nephi.

More than 700 years before the time Nephi and Jacob taught their brothers the Gospel from the Plates of Laban, Isaiah recorded in detail the events and circumstances which awaited the House of Israel. Not only did Isaiah write about the Assyrian captivity to come, but also about the Babylonian and the Roman era with its attendant persecution of the Tribe of Judah. The coming of the Christ in the meridian of time, his crucifixion and resurrection, the eventual scattering of the Jews throughout the earth, and the desolation of their land. All of these events have been literally fulfilled. History attests to the prophetic words of Isaiah, that he truly spoke what the spirit dictated and what the Lord had him make known to men.

Men are prone to argue that these events are of antiquity and little related to our own time, and so they say, "Why get excited? All is well in Zion. We have no need to fear." But Isaiah's words apply to present history as well. He saw it clearly. He was privileged to see the restoration of the Gospel, the coming forth of the records of the Nephites, and the establishment of this great gentile nation and its many and great accomplishments. He saw the persecution of the Lamanites at the hands of the gentiles, but also the eventual blessing and help received from them. He saw and told about our grandparents' day, and their trek across the plains and how they found refuge in the desert, which would rejoice at their coming and "blossom as a rose".

"Antiquity," they say. Isaiah even saw the events of today, the turmoil stirred up in our society by the influences of Lucifer and his lies, the breakdown of our moral standards, the turning away from God, the forsaking of truth. We are witnesses to these events now, and we cannot explain them away by saying "Oh, they have occurred in all ages of time and are not just of our own day." No, Isaiah gave us a spiritual and literal calendar by which we can guide our lives.

Nephi, in teaching his people from the Plates of Laban, had all of Isaiah's words. Though he did not copy all of them onto his plates, he refers to them, and he specifically refers to the words of a book that would come forth, part of which would be sealed and part to be revealed to men. All this he records in 2 Nephi 27:5-29.

Isaiah very similarly records his vision in the 29th Chapter, and in it he gives us a calendar—a more sure word of prophecy—for the days of these events.

Isaiah says that after the words of this sealed book shall come forth, which book was none other than the Book of Mormon as no other book can qualify—"Is it not yet a very little while, and Lebanon shall be turned into a fruitful field and the fruitful field shall be esteemed as a forest?" (Isaiah 29:17) This Lebanon of which Isaiah speaks is not confined to the geographic boundries of the country or nation we know as Lebanon today. It comprises all of what was given to the House of Israel as the promised land and was divided among the twelve tribes when Joshua replaced Moses and led them into the "lands of their inheritance." In brief, this was all of ancient Palestine, what is now Israel, Lebanon, and some of Jordan, and more.

Jerusalem was destroyed and the Jews were scattered to the four corners of the earth some 134 years after Christ. This land of milk and honey—this crossroads of nations, this area which had incited more controversy and more desire for possession than any comparable strip of land in the world became a land of desolation, void of commerce, of production, barren and covered by shifting sand and inhabited by roving bands of Bedouins who could barely exist on it. This was to become like a forest or to become so productive that it would support all of Judah whom the spirit would lead home to the "land of their inheritance." For over eighteen hundred years this land would be barren, but then a miracle would happen. The Lord would set his hand to gather his covenant people and prepare them for their destiny.

After the words of this sealed book came forth in 1830, Isaiah's calendar begins as a record of events which astounds the imagination and provides the evidence of happenings too numerous and too fantastic to explain away with casual logic.

In 1841 the land of Palestine was dedicated for the gathering of the Jews by a member of the tribe of Judah, Orson Hyde, an early apostle in the Church of Jesus Christ of Latter-day Saints. His dedicatory prayer promised that Great Britain would aid in this great gathering process, and that the land would literally become a land of milk and honey. What was there to base this promise on except the same spirit of prophecy that had directed Isaiah? Here are some facts, hard to explain away. In 1770, sixty years before the words of the book came forth, there were but 5,000 Jews in all of Palestine. By 1839, this number had increased to 11,000; by 1879 there were 34,000. At the close of the first World War, in 1918, Great Britain was given a mandate over the land of Palestine and thus began the rebuilding of this homeland for the Jews. There were then about 70,000 Jews in all of Palestine. The next ten years saw the population increase to some 170,000. The Jewish people had constructed 600 miles of new railroad, had built 200 village schools, had covered the denuded hills with 5,000,000 freshly planted trees, and had turned 15,000 acres of marshland into fertile farms, launched 150 new industrial undertakings. They had built dams on the Jordan River and had made available 5,000,000 tons of water every day for power generation and irrigation. By then the country was exporting $10,000,000 worth of trade mostly in farm produce, among which was 2,658,249 cases of oranges.

But the miracle had just begun. The next 30 years witnessed some troublesome times. 484,000 Jewish immigrants were admitted to Palestine, and the economy continued to grow in proportion to the populace. In May 1948, Great Britain terminated her mandate, and for the first time in more than 1,800 years, the Jews had a homeland with their own government.

In the first three and one-half years as a nation, the Jews returned to Palestine at the rate of 23 per hour, day and night, and by the end of 1953, 718,000 new immigrants had arrived in their new homeland, swelling the population to 1,650,000 by 1953.

Agriculture, which continued to be the mainstay of the economy, was now producing and exporting some 7,000,000 cases of citrus fruit as well as numerous other products. Irrigated acres increased to some 125,000 and industrial expansion increased proportionately, with exports exceeding $10,000,000 annually.

Now Israel has passed its first 20 years as a nation. It has experienced organized opposition from its neighbors. It has increased its expansion phenomenally; its populace is now approaching 3,000,000. It is a recognized nation of the world racing to its destiny—its acceptance of the Messiah in his second advent.

Israel has fought numerous battles with its adversaries. The fantastic six-day war with the Arab nations leaves one in awe and the only conclusion that can be reached is that the Lord has fulfilled the prophecies of Isaiah—that he will return Israel to the land of its inheritance, and that he will fight their battles.

Now what lesson can we learn from these fantastic events happening in our day—events that fulfill Isaiah's prophecies, which were uttered some 2,700 years ago?

We can but conclude that what Isaiah said will be truly fulfilled. We are rapidly approaching the hour of the Lord's coming. We need to be aware of our condition, we need to be engaged in a good cause, and we need to be obedient to the laws and commandments of the Lord. If we have hope of peace, safety, and freedom in this land of our inheritance, we need serve the God of this land, which is Jesus Christ.

As Isaiah's calendar of events is fulfilled, we can surely know that every word and event will be fulfilled now and in the future.

The Text of The Book of Mormon

THE SECOND BOOK OF NEPHI

An account of the death of Lehi. Nephi's brethren rebel against him. The Lord warns Nephi to depart into the wilderness. His journeyings in the wilderness, &c.

CHAPTER 1.

1.   And now it came to pass that after I, Nephi, had made an end of teaching my brethren, our father, Lehi, also spake many things unto them—how great things the Lord had done for them in bringing them out of the land of Jerusalem.

2.   And he spake unto them concerning their rebellions upon the waters, and the mercies of God in sparing their lives, that they were not swallowed up in the sea.

3.   And he also spake unto them concerning the land of promise, which they had obtained—how merciful the Lord had been in warning us that we should flee out of the land of Jerusalem.

4.   For, behold, said he, I have seen a vision, in which I know that Jerusalem is destroyed; and had we remained in Jerusalem we should also have perished.

5.   But, said he, notwithstanding our afflictions, we have obtained a land of promise, a land which is choice above all other lands; a land which the Lord God hath covenanted with me should be a land for the inheritance of my seed. Yea, the Lord hath covenanted this land unto me, and to my children forever, and also all those who should be led out of other countries by the hand of the Lord.

6.   Wherefore, I, Lehi, prophesy according to the workings of the Spirit which is in me, that there shall none come into this land save they shall be brought by the hand of the Lord.

7.   Wherefore, this land is consecrated unto him whom he shall bring. And if it so be that they shall serve him according to the commandments which he hath given, it shall be a land of liberty unto them; wherefore, they shall never be brought down into captivity; if so, it shall be because of iniquity; for if iniquity shall abound cursed shall be the land for their sakes, but unto the righteous it shall be blessed forever.

8.   And behold, it is wisdom that this land should be kept as yet from the knowledge of other nations; for behold, many nations would overrun the land, that there would be no place for an inheritance.

9.   Wherefore, I, Lehi, have obtained a promise, that inasmuch as those whom the Lord God shall bring out of the land of Jerusalem shall keep his commandments, they shall prosper upon the face of this land; and they shall be kept from all other nations, that they may possess this land unto themselves. And if it so be that they shall keep his commandments they shall be blessed upon the face of this land, and there shall be none to molest them, nor to take away the land of their inheritance; and they shall dwell safely forever.

10.   But behold, when the time cometh that they shall dwindle in unbelief, after they have received so great blessings from the hand of the Lord—having a knowledge of the creation of the earth, and all men, knowing the great and marvelous works of the Lord from the creation of the world; having power given them to do all things by faith; having all the commandments from the beginning, and having been brought by his infinite goodness into this precious land of promise—behold, I say, if the day shall come that they will reject the Holy One of Israel, the true Messiah, their Redeemer and their God, behold, the judgments of him that is just shall rest upon them.

11.   Yea, he will bring other nations unto them, and he will give unto them power, and he will take away from them the lands of their possessions, and he will cause them to be scattered and smitten.

12.   Yea, as one generation passeth to another there shall be bloodsheds, and great visitations among them; wherefore, my sons, I would that ye would remember; yea, I would that ye would hearken unto my words.

13.   O that ye would awake; awake from a deep sleep, yea, even from the sleep of hell, and shake off the awful chains by which ye are bound, which are the chains which bind the children of men, that they are carried away captive down to the eternal gulf of misery and woe.

14.   Awake! and arise from the dust, and hear the words of a trembling parent, whose limbs ye must soon lay down in the cold and silent grave, from whence no traveler can return; a few more days and I go the way of all the earth.

15.   But behold, the Lord hath redeemed my soul from hell; I have beheld his glory, and I am encircled about eternally in the arms of his love.

16.   And I desire that ye should remember to observe the statutes and the judgments of the Lord; behold, this hath been the anxiety of my soul from the beginning.

17. My heart hath been weighed down with sorrow from time to time, for I have feared, lest for the hardness of your hearts the Lord your God should come out in the fulness of his wrath upon you, that ye be cut off and destroyed forever;

18. Or, that a cursing should come upon you for the space of many generations; and ye are visited by sword, and by famine, and are hated, and are led according to the will and captivity of the devil.

19. O my sons, that these things might not come upon you, but that ye might be a choice and a favored people of the Lord. But behold, his will be done; for his ways are righteousness forever.

20. And he hath said that: Inasmuch as ye shall keep my commandments ye shall prosper in the land; but inasmuch as ye will not keep my commandments ye shall be cut off from my presence.

21. And now that my soul might have joy in you, and that my heart might leave this world with gladness because of you, that I might not be brought down with grief and sorrow to the grave, arise from the dust, my sons, and be men, and be determined in one mind and in one heart, united in all things, that ye may not come down into captivity;

22. That ye may not be cursed with a sore cursing; and also, that ye may not incur the displeasure of a just God upon you, unto the destruction, yea, the eternal destruction of both soul and body.

23. Awake, my sons; put on the armor of righteousness. Shake off the chains with which ye are bound, and come forth out of obscurity, and arise from the dust.

24. Rebel no more against your brother, whose views have been glorious, and who hath kept the commandments from the time that we left Jerusalem; and who hath been an instrument in the hands of God, in bringing us forth into the land of promise; for were it not for him, we must have perished with hunger in the wilderness; nevertheless, ye sought to take away his life; yea, and he hath suffered much sorrow because of you.

25. And I exceedingly fear and tremble because of you, lest he shall suffer again; for behold, ye have accused him that he sought power and authority over you; but I know that he hath not sought for power nor authority over you, but he hath sought the glory of God, and your own eternal welfare.

26. And ye have murmured because he hath been plain unto you. Ye say that he hath used sharpness; ye say that he hath been angry with you; but behold, his sharpness was the sharpness of the power of the word of God, which was in him; and that which ye call anger was the truth, according to that which is in God, which he could not restrain, manifesting boldly concerning your iniquities.

27. And it must needs be that the power of God must be with him, even unto his commanding you that ye must obey. But behold, it was not he, but it was the Spirit of the Lord which was in him, which opened his mouth to utterance that he could not shut it.

28. And now my son, Laman, and also Lemuel and Sam, and also my sons who are the sons of Ishmael, behold, if ye will hearken unto the voice of Nephi ye shall not perish. And if ye will hearken unto him I leave unto you a blessing, yea, even my first blessing.

29. But if ye will not hearken unto him I take away my first blessing, yea, even my blessing, and it shall rest upon him.

30. And now, Zoram, I speak unto you: Behold, thou art the servant of Laban; nevertheless, thou hast been brought out of the land of Jerusalem, and I know that thou art a true friend unto my son, Nephi, forever.

31. Wherefore, because thou hast been faithful thy seed shall be blessed with his seed, that they dwell in prosperity long upon the face of this land; and nothing, save it shall be iniquity among them, shall harm or disturb their prosperity upon the face of this land forever.

32. Wherefore, if ye shall keep the commandments of the Lord, the Lord hath consecrated this land for the security of thy seed with the seed of my son.

CHAPTER 2.

1. And now, Jacob, I speak unto you: Thou art my first-born in the days of my tribulation in the wilderness. And behold, in thy childhood thou hast suffered afflictions and much sorrow, because of the rudeness of thy brethren.

2. Nevertheless, Jacob, my first-born in the wilderness, thou knowest the greatness of God; and he shall consecrate thine afflictions for thy gain.

3. Wherefore, thy soul shall be blessed, and thou shalt dwell safely with thy brother, Nephi; and thy days shall be spent in the service of thy God. Wherefore, I know that thou art redeemed, because of the righteousness of thy Redeemer; for thou hast beheld that in the fulness of time he cometh to bring salvation unto men.

4. And thou hast beheld in thy youth his glory; wherefore, thou art blessed even as they unto whom he shall minister in the flesh; for the Spirit is the same, yesterday, today, and forever. And the way is prepared from the fall of man, and salvation is free.

5. And men are instructed sufficiently that they know good from evil. And the law is given unto men. And by the law no flesh is justified; or, by the law men are cut

off. Yea, by the temporal law they were cut off; and also, by the spiritual law they perish from that which is good, and become miserable forever.

6. Wherefore, redemption cometh in and through the Holy Messiah; for he is full of grace and truth.

7. Behold, he offereth himself a sacrifice for sin, to answer the ends of the law, unto all those who have a broken heart and a contrite spirit; and unto none else can the ends of the law be answered.

8. Wherefore, how great the importance to make these things known unto the inhabitants of the earth, that they may know that there is no flesh that can dwell in the presence of God, save it be through the merits, and mercy, and grace of the Holy Messiah, who layeth down his life according to the flesh, and taketh it again by the power of the Spirit, that he may bring to pass the resurrection of the dead, being the first that should rise.

9. Wherefore, he is the first-fruits unto God, inasmuch as he shall make intercession for all the children of men; and they that believe in him shall be saved.

10. And because of the intercession for all, all men come unto God; wherefore, they stand in the presence of him to be judged of him according to the truth and holiness which is in him. Wherefore, the ends of the law which the Holy One hath given, unto the inflicting of the punishment which is affixed, which punishment that is affixed is in opposition to that of the happiness which is affixed, to answer the ends of the atonement—

11. For it must needs be, that there is an opposition in all things. If not so, my first-born in the wilderness, righteousness could not be brought to pass, neither wickedness, neither holiness nor misery, neither good nor bad. Wherefore, all things must needs be a compound in one; wherefore, if it should be one body it must needs remain as dead, having no life neither death, nor corruption nor incorruption, happiness nor misery, neither sense nor insensibility.

12. Wherefore, it must needs have been created for a thing of naught; wherefore there would have been no purpose in the end of its creation. Wherefore, this thing must needs destroy the wisdom of God and his eternal purposes, and also the power, and the mercy, and the justice of God.

13. And if ye shall say there is no law, ye shall also say there is no sin. If ye shall say there is no sin, ye shall also say there is no righteousness. And if there be no righteousness there be no happiness. And if there be no righteousness nor happiness there be no punishment nor misery. And if these things are not there is no God. And if there is no God we are not, neither the earth; for there could have been no creation of things, neither to act nor to be acted upon; wherefore, all things must have vanished away.

14. And now, my sons, I speak unto you these things for your profit and learning; for there is a God, and he hath created all things, both the heavens and the earth, and all things that in them are, both things to act and things to be acted upon.

15. And to bring about his eternal purposes in the end of man, after he had created our first parents, and the beasts of the field and the fowls of the air, and in fine, all things which are created, it must needs be that there was an opposition; even the forbidden fruit in opposition to the tree of life; the one being sweet and the other bitter.

16. Wherefore, the Lord God gave unto man that he should act for himself. Wherefore, man could not act for himself save it should be that he was enticed by the one or the other.

17. And I, Lehi, according to the things which I have read, must needs suppose that an angel of God, according to that which is written, had fallen from heaven; wherefore, he became a devil, having sought that which was evil before God.

18. And because he had fallen from heaven, and had become miserable forever, he sought also the misery of all mankind. Wherefore, he said unto Eve, yea, even that old serpent, who is the devil, who is the father of all lies, wherefore he said: Partake of the forbidden fruit, and ye shall not die, but ye shall be as God, knowing good and evil.

19. And after Adam and Eve had partaken of the forbidden fruit they were driven out of the garden of Eden, to till the earth.

20. And they have brought forth children; yea, even the family of all the earth.

21. And the days of the children of men were prolonged, according to the will of God, that they might repent while in the flesh; wherefore, their state became a state of probation, and their time was lengthened, according to the commandments which the Lord God gave unto the children of men. For he gave commandment that all men must repent; for he showed unto all men that they were lost, because of the transgression of their parents.

22. And now, behold, if Adam had not transgressed he would not have fallen, but he would have remained in the garden of Eden. And all things which were created must have remained in the same state in which they were after they were created; and they must have remained forever, and had no end.

23. And they would have had no children; wherefore they would have remained in a state of innocence, having no joy, for they knew no misery; doing no good, for they knew no sin.

24. But behold, all things have been done in the wisdom of him who knoweth all things.

25. Adam fell that men might be; and men are, that

they might have joy.

26. And the Messiah cometh in the fulness of time, that he may redeem the children of men from the fall. And because that they are redeemed from the fall they have become free forever, knowing good from evil; to act for themselves and not to be acted upon, save it be by the punishment of the law at the great and last day, according to the commandments which God hath given.

27. Wherefore, men are free according to the flesh; and all things are given them which are expedient unto man. And they are free to choose liberty and eternal life, through the great mediation of all men, or to choose captivity and death, according to the captivity and power of the devil; for he seeketh that all men might be miserable like unto himself.

28. And now, my sons, I would that ye should look to the great Mediator, and hearken unto his great commandments; and be faithful unto his words, and choose eternal life, according to the will of his Holy Spirit;

29. And not choose eternal death, according to the will of the flesh and the evil which is therein, which giveth the spirit of the devil power to captivate, to bring you down to hell, that he may reign over you in his own kingdom.

30. I have spoken these few words unto you all, my sons, in the last days of my probation; and I have chosen the good part, according to the words of the prophet. And I have none other object save it be the everlasting welfare of your souls. Amen.

CHAPTER 3.

1. And now I speak unto you, Joseph, my last-born. Thou wast born in the wilderness of mine afflictions; yea, in the days of my greatest sorrow did thy mother bear thee.

2. And may the Lord consecrate also unto thee this land, which is a most precious land, for thine inheritance and the inheritance of thy seed with thy brethren, for thy security forever, if it so be that ye shall keep the commandments of the Holy One of Israel.

3. And now, Joseph, my last-born, whom I have brought out of the wilderness of mine afflictions, may the Lord bless thee forever, for thy seed shall not utterly be destroyed.

4. For behold, thou art the fruit of my loins; and I am a descendant of Joseph who was carried captive into Egypt. And great were the covenants of the Lord which he made unto Joseph.

5. Wherefore, Joseph truly saw our day. And he obtained a promise of the Lord, that out of the fruit of his loins the Lord God would rise up a righteous branch unto the house of Israel; not the Messiah, but a branch which was to be broken off, nevertheless, to be remembered in the covenants of the Lord that the Messiah should be made manifest unto them in the latter days, in the spirit of power, unto the bringing of them out of darkness unto light—yea, out of hidden darkness and out of captivity unto freedom.

6. For Joseph truly testified, saying: A seer shall the Lord my God raise up, who shall be a choice seer unto the fruit of my loins.

7. Yea, Joseph truly said: Thus saith the Lord unto me: A choice seer will I raise up out of the fruit of thy loins; and he shall be esteemed highly among the fruit of thy loins. And unto him will I give commandment that he shall do a work for the fruit of thy loins, his brethren, which shall be of great worth unto them, even to the bringing of them to the knowledge of the covenants which I have made with thy fathers.

8. And I will give unto him a commandment that he shall do none other work, save the work which I shall command him. And I will make him great in mine eyes; for he shall do my work.

9. And he shall be great like unto Moses, whom I have said I would raise up unto you, to deliver my people, O house of Israel.

10. And Moses will I raise up, to deliver thy people out of the land of Egypt.

11. But a seer will I raise up out of the fruit of thy loins; and unto him will I give power to bring forth my word unto the seed of thy loins—and not to the bringing forth my word only, saith the Lord, but to the convincing them of my word, which shall have already gone forth among them.

12. Wherefore, the fruit of thy loins shall write; and the fruit of the loins of Judah shall write; and that which shall be written by the fruit of thy loins, and also that which shall be written by the fruit of the loins of Judah, shall grow together, unto the confounding of false doctrines and laying down of contentions, and establishing peace among the fruit of thy loins, and bringing them to the knowledge of their fathers in the latter days, and also to the knowledge of my covenants, saith the Lord.

13. And out of weakness he shall be made strong, in that day when my work shall commence among all my people, unto the restoring thee, O house of Israel, saith the Lord.

14. And thus prophesied Joseph, saying: Behold, that seer will the Lord bless; and they that seek to destroy him shall be confounded; for this promise, which I have obtained of the Lord, of the fruit of my loins, shall be fulfilled. Behold, I am sure of the fulfilling of this promise;

15. And his name shall be called after me; and it shall be after the name of his father. And he shall be like unto me; for the thing, which the Lord shall bring forth by his hand, by the power of the Lord shall bring my people unto salvation.

16. Yea, thus prophesied Joseph: I am sure of this thing, even as I am sure of the promise of Moses; for the Lord hath said unto me, I will preserve thy seed forever.

17. And the Lord hath said: I will raise up a Moses; and I will give power unto him in a rod; and I will give judgment unto him in writing. Yet I will not loose his tongue, that he shall speak much, for I will not make him mighty in speaking. But I will write unto him my law, by the finger of mine own hand; and I will make a spokesman for him.

18. And the Lord said unto me also: I will raise up unto the fruit of thy loins; and I will make for him a spokesman. And I, behold, I will give unto him that he shall write the writing of the fruit of thy loins, unto the fruit of thy loins; and the spokesman of thy loins shall declare it.

19. And the words which he shall write shall be the words which are expedient in my wisdom should go forth unto the fruit of thy loins. And it shall be as if the fruit of thy loins had cried unto them from the dust; for I know their faith.

20. And they shall cry from the dust; yea, even repentance unto their brethren, even after many generations have gone by them. And it shall come to pass that their cry shall go, even according to the simpleness of their words.

21. Because of their faith their words shall proceed forth out of my mouth unto their brethren who are the fruit of thy loins; and the weakness of their words will I make strong in their faith, unto the remembering of my covenant which I made unto thy fathers.

22. And now, behold, my son Joseph, after this manner did my father of old prophesy.

23. Wherefore, because of this covenant thou art blessed; for thy seed shall not be destroyed, for they shall hearken unto the words of the book.

24. And there shall rise up one mighty among them, who shall do much good, both in word and in deed, being an instrument in the hands of God, with exceeding faith, to work mighty wonders, and do that thing which is great in the sight of God, unto the bringing to pass much restoration unto the house of Israel, and unto the seed of thy brethren.

25. And now, blessed art thou, Joseph. Behold, thou art little; wherefore hearken unto the words of thy brother, Nephi, and it shall be done unto thee even according to the words which I have spoken. Remember the words of thy dying father. Amen.

CHAPTER 4.

1. And now, I, Nephi, speak concerning the prophecies of which my father hath spoken, concerning Joseph, who was carried into Egypt.

2. For behold, he truly prophesied concerning all his seed. And the prophecies which he wrote, there are not many greater. And he prophesied concerning us, and our future generations; and they are written upon the plates of brass.

3. Wherefore, after my father had made an end of speaking concerning the prophecies of Joseph, he called the children of Laman, his sons, and his daughters, and said unto them: Behold, my sons, and my daughters, who are the sons and daughters of my first-born, I would that ye should give ear unto my words.

4. For the Lord God hath said that: Inasmuch as ye shall keep my commandments ye shall prosper in the land; and inasmuch as ye will not keep my commandments ye shall be cut off from my presence.

5. But behold, my sons and my daughters, I cannot go down to my grave save I should leave a blessing upon you; for behold, I know that if ye are brought up in the way ye should go ye will not depart from it.

6. Wherefore, if ye are cursed, behold, I leave my blessing upon you, that the cursing may be taken from you and be answered upon the heads of your parents.

7. Wherefore, because of my blessing the Lord God will not suffer that ye shall perish; wherefore, he will be merciful unto you and unto your seed forever.

8. And it came to pass that after my father had made an end of speaking to the sons and daughters of Laman, he caused the sons and daughters of Lemuel to be brought before him.

9. And he spake unto them, saying: Behold, my sons and my daughters, who are the sons and the daughters of my second son; behold I leave unto you the same blessing which I left unto the sons and daughters of Laman; wherefore, thou shalt not utterly be destroyed; but in the end thy seed shall be blessed.

10. And it came to pass that when my father had made an end of speaking unto them, behold, he spake unto the sons of Ishmael, yea, and even all his household.

11. And after he had made an end of speaking unto them, he spake unto Sam, saying: Blessed art thou, and thy seed; for thou shall inherit the land like unto thy brother Nephi. And thy seed shall be numbered with his seed; and thou shalt be even like unto thy brother, and thy seed like unto his seed; and thou shalt be blessed in all thy days.

12. And it came to pass after my father, Lehi, had spoken unto all his household, according to the feelings of his heart and the Spirit of the Lord which was in him, he

waxed old. And it came to pass that he died, and was buried.

13. And it came to pass that not many days after his death, Laman and Lemuel and the sons of Ishmael were angry with me because of the admonitions of the Lord.

14. For I, Nephi, was constrained to speak unto them, according to his word; for I had spoken many things unto them, and also my father, before his death; many of which sayings are written upon mine other plates; for a more history part are written upon mine other plates.

15. And upon these I write the things of my soul, and many of the scriptures which are engraven upon the plates of brass. For my soul delighteth in the scriptures, and my heart pondereth them, and writeth them for the learning and the profit of my children.

16. Behold, my soul delighteth in the things of the Lord; and my heart pondereth continually upon the things which I have seen and heard.

17. Nevertheless, notwithstanding the great goodness of the Lord, in showing me his great and marvelous works, my heart exclaimeth: O wretched man that I am! Yea, my heart sorroweth because of my flesh; my soul grieveth because of mine iniquities.

18. I am encompassed about, because of the temptations and the sins which do so easily beset me.

19. And when I desire to rejoice, my heart groaneth because of my sins; nevertheless, I know in whom I have trusted.

20. My God hath been my support; he hath led me through mine afflictions in the wilderness; and he hath preserved me upon the waters of the great deep.

21. He hath filled me with his love, even unto the consuming of my flesh.

22. He hath confounded mine enemies, unto the causing of them to quake before me.

23. Behold, he hath heard my cry by day, and he hath given me knowledge by visions in the nighttime.

24. And by day have I waxed bold in mighty prayer before him; yea, my voice have I sent up on high; and angels came down and ministered unto me.

25. And upon the wings of his Spirit hath my body been carried away upon exceeding high mountains. And mine eyes have beheld great things, yea, even too great for man; therefore I was bidden that I should not write them.

26. O then, if I have seen so great things, if the Lord in his condescension unto the children of men hath visited men in so much mercy, why should my heart weep and my soul linger in the valley of sorrow, and my flesh waste away, and my strength slacken, because of mine afflictions?

27. And why should I yield to sin, because of my flesh? Yea, why should I give way to temptations, that the evil one have place in my heart to destroy my peace and afflict my soul? Why am I angry because of mine enemy?

28. Awake, my soul! No longer droop in sin. Rejoice, O my heart, and give place no more for the enemy of my soul.

29. Do not anger again because of mine enemies. Do not slacken my strength because of mine afflictions.

30. Rejoice, O my heart, and cry unto the Lord, and say: O Lord, I will praise thee forever; yea, my soul will rejoice in thee, my God, and the rock of my salvation.

31. O Lord, wilt thou redeem my soul? Wilt thou deliver me out of the hands of mine enemies? Wilt thou make me that I may shake at the appearance of sin?

32. May the gates of hell be shut continually before me, because that my heart is broken and my spirit is contrite! O Lord, wilt thou not shut the gates of thy righteousness before me, that I may walk in the path of the low valley, that I may be strict in the plain road!

33. O Lord, wilt thou encircle me around in the robe of thy righteousness! O Lord, wilt thou make a way for mine escape before mine enemies! Wilt thou make my path staight before me! Wilt thou not place a stumbling block in my way—but that thou wouldst clear my way before me, and hedge not up my way, but the ways of mine enemy.

34. O Lord, I have trusted in thee, and I will trust in thee forever. I will not put my trust in the arm of flesh; for I know that cursed is he that putteth his trust in the arm of flesh. Yea, cursed is he that putteth his trust in man or maketh flesh his arm.

35. Yea, I know that God will give liberally to him that asketh. Yea, my God will give me, if I ask not amiss; therefore I will lift up my voice unto thee; yea, I will cry unto thee, my God, the rock of my righteousness. Behold, my voice shall forever ascend up unto thee, my rock and mine everlasting God. Amen.

CHAPTER 5.

1. Behold, it came to pass that I, Nephi, did cry much unto the Lord my God, because of the anger of my brethren.

2. But behold, their anger did increase against me, insomuch that they did seek to take away my life.

3. Yea, they did murmur against me, saying: Our younger brother thinks to rule over us; and we have had much trial because of him; wherefore, now let us slay him, that we may not be afflicted more because of his words. For behold, we will not have him to be our ruler; for it belongs unto us, who are the elder brethren, to rule over this people.

4. Now I do not write upon these plates all the words which they murmured against me. But it sufficeth me to say, that they did seek to take away my life.

5. And it came to pass that the Lord did warn me, that I, Nephi, should depart from them and flee into the wilderness, and all those who would go with me.

6. Wherefore, it came to pass that I, Nephi, did take my family, and also Zoram and his family, and Sam, mine elder brother and his family, and Jacob and Joseph, my younger brethren, and also my sisters, and all those who would go with me. And all those who would go with me were those who believed in the warnings and the revelations of God; wherefore, they did hearken unto my words.

7. And we did take our tents and whatsoever things were possible for us, and did journey in the wilderness for the space of many days. And after we had journeyed for the space of many days we did pitch our tents.

8. And my people would that we should call the name of the place Nephi; wherefore, we did call it Nephi.

9. And all those who were with me did take upon them to call themselves the people of Nephi.

10. And we did observe to keep the judgments, and the statutes, and the commandments of the Lord in all things according to the law of Moses.

11. And the Lord was with us; and we did prosper exceedingly; for we did sow seed, and we did reap again in abundance. And we began to raise flocks, and herds, and animals of every kind.

12. And I, Nephi, had also brought the records which were engraven upon the plates of brass; and also the ball, or compass, which was prepared for my father by the hand of the Lord, according to that which is written.

13. And it came to pass that we began to prosper exceedingly, and to multiply in the land.

14. And I, Nephi, did take the sword of Laban, and after the manner of it did make many swords, lest by any means the people who were now called Lamanites should come upon us and destroy us; for I knew their hatred towards me and my children and those who were called my people.

15. And I did teach my people to build buildings, and to work in all manner of wood, and of iron, and of copper, and of brass, and of steel, and of gold, and of silver, and of precious ores, which were in great abundance.

16. And I, Nephi, did build a temple; and I did construct it after the manner of the temple of Solomon save it were not built of so many precious things; for they were not to be found upon the land, wherefore, it could not be built like unto Solomon's temple. But the manner of the construction was like unto the temple of Solomon; and the workmanship thereof was exceeding fine.

17. And it came to pass that I, Nephi, did cause my people to be industrious, and to labor with their hands.

18. And it came to pass that they would that I should be their king. But I, Nephi, was desirous that they should have no king; nevertheless, I did for them according to that which was in my power.

19. And behold, the words of the Lord had been fulfilled unto my brethren, which he spake concerning them, that I should be their ruler and their teacher. Wherefore, I had been their ruler and their teacher, according to the commandments of the Lord, until the time they sought to take away my life.

20. Wherefore, the word of the Lord was fulfilled which he spake unto me, saying that: Inasmuch as they will not hearken unto thy words they shall be cut off from the presence of the Lord. And behold, they were cut off from his presence.

21. And he had caused the cursing to come upon them, yea, even a sore cursing, because of their iniquity. For behold, they had hardened their hearts against him, that they had become like unto a flint; wherefore, as they were white, and exceeding fair and delightsome, that they might not be enticing unto my people the Lord God did cause a skin of blackness to come upon them.

22. And thus saith the Lord God: I will cause that they shall be loathsome unto thy people, save they shall repent of their iniquities.

23. And cursed shall be the seed of him that mixeth with their seed; for they shall be cursed even with the same cursing. And the Lord spake it, and it was done.

24. And because of their cursing which was upon them they did become an idle people, full of mischief and subtlety, and did seek in the wilderness for beasts of prey.

25. And the Lord God said unto me: They shall be a scourge unto thy seed, to stir them up in remembrance of me; and inasmuch as they will not remember me, and hearken unto my words, they shall scourge them even unto destruction.

26. And it came to pass that I, Nephi, did consecrate Jacob and Joseph, that they should be priests and teachers over the land of my people.

27. And it came to pass that we lived after the manner of happiness.

28. And thirty years had passed away from the time we left Jerusalem.

29. And I, Nephi, had kept the records upon my plates, which I had made, of my people thus far.

30. And it came to pass that the Lord God said unto me: Make other plates; and thou shalt engraven many things upon them which are good in my sight, for the profit of thy people.

31. Wherefore, I, Nephi, to be obedient to the commandments of the Lord, went and made these plates upon which I have engraven these things.

32. And I engraved that which is pleasing unto God. And if my people are pleased with the things of God they

will be pleased with mine engravings which are upon these plates.

33. And if my people desire to know the more particular part of the history of my people they must search mine other plates.

34. And it sufficeth me to say that forty years had passed away, and we had already had wars and contentions with our brethren.

CHAPTER 6.

1. The words of Jacob, the brother of Nephi, which he spake unto the people of Nephi:

2. Behold, my beloved brethren, I, Jacob, having been called of God, and ordained after the manner of his holy order, and having been consecrated by my brother Nephi, unto whom ye look as a king or a protector, and on whom ye depend for safety, behold ye know that I have spoken unto you exceeding many things.

3. Nevertheless, I speak unto you again; for I am desirous for the welfare of your souls. Yea, mine anxiety is great for you; and ye yourselves know that it ever has been. For I have exhorted you with all diligence; and I have taught you the words of my father; and I have spoken unto you concerning all things which are written, from the creation of the world.

4. And now, behold, I would speak unto you concerning things which are, and which are to come; wherefore, I will read you the words of Isaiah. And they are the words which my brother has desired that I should speak unto you. And I speak unto you for your sakes, that ye may learn and glorify the name of your God.

5. And now, the words which I shall read are they which Isaiah spake concerning all the house of Israel; wherefore, they may be likened unto you, for ye are of the house of Israel. And there are many things which have been spoken by Isaiah which may be likened unto you, because ye are of the house of Israel.

6. And now these are the words: Thus saith the Lord God: Behold, I will lift up mine hand to the Gentiles, and set up my standard to the people; and they shall bring thy sons in their arms, and thy daughters shall be carried upon their shoulders.

7. And kings shall be thy nursing fathers, and their queens thy nursing mothers; they shall bow down to thee with their faces towards the earth, and lick up the dust of thy feet; and thou shalt know that I am the Lord; for they shall not be ashamed that wait for me.

8. And now I, Jacob, would speak somewhat concerning these words. For behold, the Lord has shown me that those who were at Jerusalem, from whence we came, have been slain and carried away captive.

9. Nevertheless, the Lord has shown unto me that they should return again. And he also has shown unto me that the Lord God, the Holy One of Israel, should manifest himself unto them in the flesh; and after he should manifest himself they should scourge him and crucify him, according to the words of the angel who spake it unto me.

10. And after they have hardened their hearts and stiffened their necks against the Holy One of Israel, behold, the judgments of the Holy One of Israel shall come upon them. And the day cometh that they shall be smitten and afflicted.

11. Wherefore, after they are driven to and fro, for thus saith the angel, many shall be afflicted in the flesh, and shall not be suffered to perish, because of the prayers of the faithful; they shall be scattered, and smitten, and hated; nevertheless, the Lord will be merciful unto them, that when they shall come to the knowledge of their Redeemer, they shall be gathered together again to the lands of their inheritance.

12. And blessed are the Gentiles, they of whom the prophet has written; for behold, if it so be that they shall repent and fight not against Zion, and do not unite themselves to that great and abominable church, they shall be saved; for the Lord God will fulfil his covenants which he has made unto his children; and for this cause the prophet has written these things.

13. Wherefore, they that fight against Zion and the covenant people of the Lord shall lick up the dust of their feet; and the people of the Lord shall not be ashamed. For the people of the Lord are they who wait for him; for they still wait for the coming of the Messiah.

14. And behold, according to the words of the prophet, the Messiah will set himself again the second time to recover them; wherefore, he will manifest himself unto them in power and great glory, unto the destruction of their enemies, when that day cometh when they shall believe in him; and none will he destroy that believe in him.

15. And they that believe not in him shall be destroyed, both by fire, and by tempest, and by earthquakes, and by bloodsheds, and by pestilence, and by famine. And they shall know that the Lord is God, the Holy One of Israel.

16. For shall the prey be taken from the mighty, or the lawful captive delivered?

17. But thus saith the Lord: Even the captives of the mighty shall be taken away, and the prey of the terrible shall be delivered; for the Mighty God shall deliver his covenant people. For thus saith the Lord: I will contend with them that contendeth with thee—

18. And I will feed them that oppress thee, with their

own flesh; and they shall be drunken with their own blood as with sweet wine; and all flesh shall know that I the Lord am thy Savior and thy Redeemer, the Mighty One of Jacob.

CHAPTER 7.

1. Yea, for thus saith the Lord: Have I put thee away, or have I cast thee off forever? For thus saith the Lord: Where is the bill of your mother's divorcement? To whom have I put thee away, or to which of my creditors have I sold you? Yea, to whom have I sold you? Behold, for your iniquities have ye sold yourselves, and for your transgressions is your mother put away.

2. Wherefore, when I came, there was no man; when I called, yea, there was none to answer. O house of Israel, is my hand shortened at all that it cannot redeem, or have I no power to deliver? Behold, at my rebuke I dry up the sea, I make their rivers a wilderness and their fish to stink because the waters are dried up, and they die because of thirst.

3. I clothe the heavens with blackness, and I make sackcloth their covering.

4. The Lord God hath given me the tongue of the learned, that I should know how to speak a word in season unto thee, O house of Israel. When ye are weary he waketh morning by morning. He waketh mine ear to hear as the learned.

5. The Lord God hath opened mine ear, and I was not rebellious, neither turned away back.

6. I gave my back to the smiter, and my cheeks to them that plucked off the hair. I hid not my face from shame and spitting.

7. For the Lord God will help me, therefore shall I not be confounded. Therefore have I set my face like a flint, and I know that I shall not be ashamed.

8. And the Lord is near, and he justifieth me. Who will contend with me? Let us stand together. Who is mine adversary? Let him come near me, and I will smite him with the strength of my mouth.

9. For the Lord God will help me. And all they who shall condemn me, behold, all they shall wax old as a garment, and the moth shall eat them up.

10. Who is among you that feareth the Lord, that obeyeth the voice of his servant, that walketh in darkness and hath no light?

11. Behold all ye that kindle fire, that compass yourselves about with sparks, walk in the light of your fire and in the sparks which ye have kindled. This shall ye have of mine hand—ye shall lie down in sorrow.

CHAPTER 8.

1. Hearken unto me, ye that follow after righteousness. Look unto the rock from whence ye are hewn, and to the hole of the pit from whence ye are digged.

2. Look unto Abraham, your father, and unto Sarah, she that bare you; for I called him alone, and blessed him.

3. For the Lord shall comfort Zion, he will comfort all her waste places; and he will make her wilderness like Eden, and her desert like the garden of the Lord. Joy and gladness shall be found therein, thanksgiving and the voice of melody.

4. Hearken unto me, my people; and give ear unto me, O my nation; for a law shall proceed from me, and I will make my judgment to rest for a light for the people.

5. My righteousness is near; my salvation is gone forth, and mine arm shall judge the people. The isles shall wait upon me, and on mine arm shall they trust.

6. Lift up your eyes to the heavens, and look upon the earth beneath; for the heavens shall vanish away like smoke, and the earth shall wax old like a garment; and they that dwell therein shall die in like manner. But my salvation shall be forever, and my righteousness shall not be abolished.

7. Hearken unto me, ye that know righteousness, the people in whose heart I have written my law, fear ye not the reproach of men, neither be ye afraid of their revilings.

8. For the moth shall eat them up like a garment, and the worm shall eat them like wool. But my righteousness shall be forever, and my salvation from generation to generation.

9. Awake, awake! Put on strength, O arm of the Lord; awake as in the ancient days. Art thou not he that hath cut Rahab, and wounded the dragon?

10. Art thou not he who hath dried the sea, the waters of the great deep; that hath made the depths of the sea a way for the ransomed to pass over?

11. Therefore, the redeemed of the Lord shall return, and come with singing unto Zion; and everlasting joy and holiness shall be upon their heads; and they shall obtain gladness and joy; sorrow and mourning shall flee away.

12. I am he; yea, I am he that comforteth you. Behold, who art thou, that thou shouldst be afraid of man, who shall die, and of the son of man, who shall be made like unto grass?

13. And forgettest the Lord thy maker, that hath stretched forth the heavens, and laid the foundations of the earth, and hast feared continually every day, because of the fury of the oppressor, as if he were ready to destroy? And where is the fury of the oppressor?

14. The captive exile hasteneth, that he may be loosed, and that he should not die in the pit, nor that his bread should fail.

15. But I am the Lord thy God, whose waves roared; the Lord of Hosts is my name.

16. And I have put my words in thy mouth, and have covered thee in the shadow of mine hand, that I may plant the heavens and lay the foundations of the earth, and say unto Zion: Behold, thou art my people.

17. Awake, awake, stand up, O Jerusalem, which hast drunk at the hand of the Lord the cup of his fury—thou hast drunken the dregs of the cup of trembling wrung out—

18. And none to guide her among all the sons she hath brought forth; neither that taketh her by the hand, of all the sons she hath brought up.

19. These two sons are come unto thee, who shall be sorry for thee—thy desolation and destruction, and the famine and the sword—and by whom shall I comfort thee?

20. Thy sons have fainted, save these two; they lie at the head of all the streets; as a wild bull in a net, they are full of the fury of the Lord, the rebuke of thy God.

21. Therefore hear now this, thou afflicted, and drunken, and not with wine:

22. Thus saith thy Lord, the Lord and thy God pleadeth the cause of his people; behold, I have taken out of thine hand the cup of trembling, the dregs of the cup of my fury; thou shalt no more drink it again.

23. But I will put it into the hand of them that afflict thee; who have said to thy soul: Bow down, that we may go over—and thou hast laid thy body as the ground and as the street to them that went over.

24. Awake, awake, put on thy strength, O Zion; put on thy beautiful garments, O Jerusalem, the holy city; for henceforth there shall no more come into thee the uncircumcised and the unclean.

25. Shake thyself from the dust; arise, sit down, O Jerusalem; loose thyself from the bands of thy neck, O captive daughter of Zion.

CHAPTER 9.

1. And now, my beloved brethren, I have read these things that ye might know concerning the covenants of the Lord that he has covenanted with all the house of Israel—

2. That he has spoken unto the Jews, by the mouth of his holy prophets, even from the beginning down, from generation to generation, until the time comes that they shall be restored to the true church and fold of God; when they shall be gathered home to the lands of their inheritance, and shall be established in all their lands of promise.

3. Behold, my beloved brethren, I speak unto you these things that ye may rejoice, and lift up your heads forever, because of the blessings which the Lord God shall bestow upon your children.

4. For I know that ye have searched much, many of you, to know of things to come; wherefore I know that ye know that our flesh must waste away and die; nevertheless, in our bodies we shall see God.

5. Yea, I know that ye know that in the body he shall show himself unto those at Jerusalem, from whence we came; for it is expedient that it should be among them; for it behooveth the great Creator that he suffereth himself to become subject unto man in the flesh, and die for all men, that all men might become subject unto him.

6. For as death hath passed upon all men, to fulfil the merciful plan of the great Creator, there must needs be a power of resurrection, and the resurrection must needs come unto man by reason of the fall; and the fall came by reason of transgression; and because man became fallen they were cut off from the presence of the Lord.

7. Wherefore, it must needs be an infinite atonement—save it should be an infinite atonement this corruption could not put on incorruption. Wherefore, the first judgment which came upon man must needs have remained to an endless duration. And if so, this flesh must have laid down to rot and to crumble to its mother earth, to rise no more.

8. O the wisdom of God, his mercy and grace! For behold, if the flesh should rise no more our spirits must become subject to that angel who fell from before the presence of the Eternal God, and became the devil, to rise no more.

9. And our spirits must have become like unto him, and we become devils, angels to a devil, to be shut out from the presence of our God, and to remain with the father of lies, in misery, like unto himself; yea, to that being who beguiled our first parents, who transformeth himself nigh unto an angel of light, and stirreth up the children of men unto secret combinations of murder and all manner of secret works of darkness.

10. O how great the goodness of our God, who prepareth a way for our escape from the grasp of this awful monster; yea, that monster, death and hell, which I call the death of the body, and also the death of the spirit.

11. And because of the way of deliverance of our God, the Holy One of Israel, this death, of which I have spoken, which is the temporal, shall deliver up its dead; which death is the grave.

12. And this death of which I have spoken, which is the spiritual death, shall deliver up its dead; which spiritual death is hell; wherefore, death and hell must deliver up their dead, and hell must deliver up its captive spirits, and the grave must deliver up its captive bodies, and the bodies and the spirits of men will be restored one to the other; and it is by the power of the resurrection of the Holy One of Israel.

13. O how great the plan of our God! For on the other hand, the paradise of God must deliver up the spirits of the righteous, and the grave deliver up the body of the righteous; and the spirit and the body is restored to itself again, and all men become incorruptible, and immortal, and they are living souls, having a perfect knowledge like unto us in the flesh, save it be that our knowledge shall be perfect.

14. Wherefore, we shall have a perfect knowledge of all our guilt, and our uncleanness, and our nakedness; and the righteous shall have a perfect knowledge of their enjoyment, and their righteousness, being clothed with purity, yea, even with the robe of righteousness.

15. And it shall come to pass that when all men shall have passed from this first death unto life, insomuch as they have become immortal, they must appear before the judgment-seat of the Holy One of Israel; and then cometh the judgment, and then must they be judged according to the holy judgment of God.

16. And assuredly, as the Lord liveth, for the Lord God hath spoken it, and it is his eternal word, which cannot pass away, that they who are righteous shall be righteous still, and they who are filthy shall be filthy still; wherefore, they who are filthy are the devil and his angels; and they shall go away into everlasting fire; prepared for them; and their torment is as a lake of fire and brimstone, whose flame ascendeth up forever and ever and has no end.

17. O the greatness and the justice of our God! For he executeth all his words, and they have gone forth out of his mouth, and his law must be fulfilled.

18. But, behold, the righteous, the saints of the Holy One of Israel, they who have believed in the Holy One of Israel, they who have endured the crosses of the world, and despised the shame of it, they shall inherit the kingdom of God, which was prepared for them from the foundation of the world, and their joy shall be full forever.

19. O the greatness of the mercy of our God, the Holy One of Israel! For he delivereth his saints from that awful monster the devil, and death, and hell, and that lake of fire and brimstone, which is endless torment.

20. O how great the holiness of our God! For he knoweth all things, and there is not anything save he knows it.

21. And he cometh into the world that he may save all men if they will hearken unto his voice; for behold, he suffereth the pains of all men, yea, the pains of every living creature, both men, women, and children, who belong to the family of Adam.

22. And he suffereth this that the resurrection might pass upon all men, that all might stand before him at the great and judgment day.

23. And he commandeth all men that they must repent, and be baptized in his name, having perfect faith in the Holy One of Israel, or they cannot be saved in the kingdom of God.

24. And if they will not repent and believe in his name, and be baptized in his name, and endure to the end, they must be damned; for the Lord God, the Holy One of Israel, hath spoken it.

25. Wherefore, he has given a law; and where there is no law given there is no punishment; and where there is no punishment there is no condemnation; and where there is no condemnation the mercies of the Holy One of Israel have claim upon them, because of the atonement; for they are delivered by the power of him.

26. For the atonement satisfieth the demands of his justice upon all those who have not the law given to them, that they are delivered from that awful monster, death and hell, and the devil, and the lake of fire and brimstone, which is endless torment; and they are restored to that God who gave them breath, which is the Holy One of Israel.

27. But wo unto him that has the law given, yea, that has all the commandments of God, like unto us, and that transgresseth them, and that wasteth the days of his probation, for awful is his state!

28. O that cunning plan of the evil one! O the vainness, and the frailties, and the foolishness of men! When they are learned they think they are wise, and they hearken not unto the counsel of God, for they set it aside, supposing they know of themselves, wherefore, their wisdom is foolishness and it profiteth them not. And they shall perish.

29. But to be learned is good if they hearken unto the counsels of God.

30. But wo unto the rich, who are rich as to the things of the world. For because they are rich they despise the poor, and they persecute the meek, and their hearts are upon their treasures; wherefore, their treasure is their God. And behold, their treasure shall perish with them also.

31. And wo unto the deaf that will not hear; for they shall perish.

32. Wo unto the blind that will not see; for they shall perish also.

33. Wo unto the uncircumcised of heart, for a knowledge of their iniquities shall smite them at the last day.

34. Wo unto the liar, for he shall be thrust down to hell.

35. Wo unto the murderer who deliberately killeth, for he shall die.

36. Wo unto them who commit whoredoms, for they shall be thrust down to hell.

37. Yea, wo unto those that worship idols, for the devil of all devils delighteth in them.

38. And, in fine, wo unto all those who die in their sins; for they shall return to God, and behold his face, and remain in their sins.

39. O, my beloved brethren, remember the awful-

ness in transgressing against that Holy God, and also the awfulness of yielding to the enticings of that cunning one. Remember, to be carnally-minded is death, and to be spiritually-minded is life eternal.

40. O, my beloved brethren, give ear to my words. Remember the greatness of the Holy One of Israel. Do not say that I have spoken hard things against you; for if ye do, ye will revile against the truth; for I have spoken the words of your Maker. I know that the words of truth are hard against all uncleanness; but the righteous fear them not, for they love the truth and are not shaken.

41. O then, my beloved brethren, come unto the Lord, the Holy One. Remember that his paths are righteous. Behold, the way for man is narrow, but it lieth in a straight course before him, and the keeper of the gate is the Holy One of Israel; and he employeth no servant there; and there is none other way save it be by the gate; for he cannot be deceived, for the Lord God is his name.

42. And whoso knocketh, to him will he open; and the wise, and the learned, and they that are rich, who are puffed up because of their learning, and their wisdom, and their riches—yea, they are they whom he despiseth; and save they shall cast these things away, and consider themselves fools before God, and come down in the depths of humility, he will not open unto them.

43. But the things of the wise and the prudent shall be hid from them forever—yea, that happiness which is prepared for the saints.

44. O, my beloved brethren, remember my words. Behold, I take off my garments, and I shake them before you; I pray the God of my salvation that he view me with his all-searching eye; wherefore, ye shall know at the last day, when all men shall be judged of their works, that the God of Israel did witness that I shook your iniquities from my soul, and that I stand with brightness before him, and am rid of your blood.

45. O, my beloved brethren, turn away from your sins; shake off the chains of him that would bind you fast; come unto that God who is the rock of your salvation.

46. Prepare your souls for that glorious day when justice shall be adminstered unto the righteous, even the day of judgment, that ye may not shrink with awful fear; that ye may not remember your awful guilt in perfectness, and be constrained to exclaim: Holy, holy are thy judgments, O Lord God Almighty—but I know my guilt; I trangressed thy law, and my transgressions are mine; and the devil hath obtained me, that I am a prey to his awful misery.

47. But behold, my brethren, is it expedient that I should awake you to an awful reality of these things? Would I harrow up your souls if your minds were pure? Would I

be plain unto you according to the plainness of the truth if ye were freed from sin?

48. Behold, if ye were holy I would speak unto you of holiness; but as ye are not holy, and ye look upon me as a teacher, it must needs be expedient that I teach you the consequences of sin.

49. Behold, my soul abhorreth sin, and my heart delighteth in righteousness; and I will praise the holy name of my God.

50. Come, my brethren, every one that thirsteth, come ye to the waters; and he that hath no money, come buy and eat; yea, come buy wine and milk without money and without price.

51. Wherefore, do not spend money for that which is of no worth, nor your labor for that which cannot satisfy. Hearken diligently unto me, and remember the words which I have spoken; and come unto the Holy One of Israel, and feast upon that which perisheth not, neither can be corrupted, and let your soul delight in fatness.

52. Behold, my beloved brethren, remember the words of your God; pray unto him continually by day, and give thanks unto his holy name by night. Let your hearts rejoice.

53. And behold how great the covenants of the Lord, and how great his condescensions unto the children of men; and because of his greatness, and his grace and mercy, he has promised unto us that our seed shall not utterly be destroyed, according to the flesh, but that he would preserve them; and in future generations they shall become a righteous branch unto the house of Israel.

54. And now, my brethren, I would speak unto you more; but on the morrow I will declare unto you the remainder of my words. Amen.

CHAPTER 10.

1. And now I, Jacob, speak unto you again, my beloved brethren, concerning this righteous branch of which I have spoken.

2. For behold, the promises which we have obtained are promises unto us according to the flesh; wherefore, as it has been shown unto me that many of our children shall perish in the flesh because of unbelief, nevertheless, God will be merciful unto many; and our children shall be restored, that they may come to that which will give them the true knowledge of their Redeemer.

3. Wherefore, as I said unto you, it must needs be expedient that Christ—for in the last night the angel spake unto me that this should be his name—should come among

the Jews, among those who are the more wicked part of the world; and they shall crucify him—for thus it behooveth our God, and there is none other nation on earth that would crucify their God.

4. For should the mighty miracles be wrought among other nations they would repent, and know that he be their God.

5. But because of priestcrafts and iniquities, they at Jerusalem will stiffen their necks against him, that he be crucified.

6. Wherefore, because of their iniquities, destructions, famines, pestilences, and bloodshed shall come upon them; and they who shall not be destroyed shall be scattered among all nations.

7. But behold, thus saith the Lord God: When the day cometh that they shall believe in me, that I am Christ, then have I covenanted with their fathers that they shall be restored in the flesh, upon the earth, unto the lands of their inheritance.

8. And it shall come to pass that they shall be gathered in from their long dispersion, from the isles of the sea, and from the four parts of the earth; and the nations of the Gentiles shall be great in the eyes of me, saith God, in carrying them forth to the lands of their inheritance.

9. Yea, the kings of the Gentiles shall be nursing fathers unto them, and their queens shall become nursing mothers; wherefore, the promises of the Lord are great unto the Gentiles, for he hath spoken it, and who can dispute?

10. But behold, this land, said God, shall be a land of thine inheritance, and the Gentiles shall be blessed upon the land.

11. And this land shall be a land of liberty unto the Gentiles, and there shall be no kings upon the land, who shall raise up unto the Gentiles.

12. And I will fortify this land against all other nations.

13. And he that fighteth against Zion shall perish, saith God.

14. For he that raiseth up a king against me shall perish, for I, the Lord, the king of heaven, will be their king, and I will be a light unto them forever, that hear my words.

15. Wherefore, for this cause, that my covenants may be fulfilled which I have made unto the children of men, that I will do unto them while they are in the flesh, I must needs destroy the secret works of darkness, and of murders, and of abominations.

16. Wherefore, he that fighteth against Zion, both Jew and Gentile, both bond and free, both male and female, shall perish; for they are they who are the whore of all the earth; for they who are not for me are against me, saith our God.

17. For I will fulfil my promises which I have made unto the children of men, that I will do unto them while they are in the flesh—

18. Wherefore, my beloved brethren, thus saith our God: I will afflict thy seed by the hand of the Gentiles; nevertheless, I will soften the hearts of the Gentiles, that they shall be like unto a father to them; wherefore, the Gentiles shall be blessed and numbered among the house of Israel.

19. Wherefore, I will consecrate this land unto thy seed, and them who shall be numbered among thy seed, forever, for the land of their inheritance; for it is a choice land, saith God unto me, above all other lands, wherefore I will have all men that dwell thereon that they shall worship me, saith God.

20. And now, my beloved brethren, seeing that our merciful God has given us so great knowledge concerning these things, let us remember him, and lay aside our sins, and not hang down our heads, for we are not cast off; nevertheless, we have been driven out of the land of our inheritance; but we have been led to a better land, for the Lord has made the sea our path, and we are upon an isle of the sea.

21. But great are the promises of the Lord unto them who are upon the isles of the sea; wherefore as it says isles, there must needs be more than this, and they are inhabited also by our brethren.

22. For behold, the Lord God has led away from time to time from the house of Israel, according to his will and pleasure. And now behold, the Lord remembereth all them who have been broken off, wherefore he remembereth us also.

23. Therefore, cheer up your hearts, and remember that ye are free to act for yourselves—to choose the way of everlasting death or the way of eternal life.

24. Wherefore, my beloved brethren, reconcile yourselves to the will of God, and not to the will of the devil and the flesh; and remember, after ye are reconciled unto God, that it is only in and through the grace of God that ye are saved.

25. Wherefore, may God raise you from death by the power of the resurrection, and also from everlasting death by the power of the atonement, that ye may be received into the eternal kingdom of God, that ye may praise him through grace divine. Amen.

CHAPTER 11.

1. And now, Jacob spake many more things to my people at that time; nevertheless only these things have I caused to be written, for the things which I have written sufficeth me.

2. And now I, Nephi, write more of the words of Isaiah, for my soul delighteth in his words. For I will liken his words unto my people, and I will send them forth unto all my children, for he verily saw my Redeemer, even as I have seen him.

3. And my brother, Jacob, also has seen him as I have seen him; wherefore, I will send their words forth unto my children to prove unto them that my words are true. Wherefore, by the words of three, God hath said, I will establish my word. Nevertheless, God sendeth more witnesses, and he proveth all his words.

4. Behold, my soul delighteth in proving unto my people the truth of the coming of Christ; for, for this end hath the law of Moses been given; and all things which have been given of God from the beginning of the world, unto man, are the typifying of him.

5. And also my soul delighteth in the covenants of the Lord which he hath made to our fathers; yea, my soul delighteth in his grace, and in his justice, and power, and mercy in the great and eternal plan of deliverance from death.

6. And my soul delighteth in proving unto my people that save Christ should come all men must perish.

7. For if there be no Christ there be no God; and if there be no God we are not, for there could have been no creation. But there is a God, and he is Christ, and he cometh in the fulness of his own time.

8. And now I write some of the words of Isaiah, that whoso of my people shall see these words may lift up their hearts and rejoice for all men. Now these are the words, and ye may liken them unto you and unto all men.

CHAPTER 12.

1. The word that Isaiah, the son of Amoz, saw concerning Judah and Jerusalem:

2. And it shall come to pass in the last days, when the mountain of the Lord's house shall be established in the top of the mountains, and shall be exalted above the hills, and all nations shall flow unto it.

3. And many people shall go and say, Come ye, and let us go up to the mountain the Lord, to the house of the God of Jacob; and he will teach us of his ways, and we will walk in his paths; for out of Zion shall go forth the law, and the word of the Lord from Jerusalem.

4. And he shall judge among the nations, and shall rebuke many people: and they shall beat their swords into plow-shares, and their spears into pruning-hooks—nation shall not lift up sword against nation, neither shall they learn war any more.

5. O house of Jacob, come ye and let us walk in the light of the Lord; yea, come, for ye have all gone astray, every one to his wicked ways.

6. Therefore, O Lord, thou hast forsaken thy people, the house of Jacob, because they be replenished from the east, and hearken unto soothsayers like the Philistines, and they please themselves in the children of strangers.

7. Their land also is full of silver and gold, neither is there any end of their treasures; their land is also full of horses, neither is there any end of their chariots.

8. Their land is also full of idols; they worship the work of their own hands, that which their own fingers have made.

9. And the mean man boweth not down, and the great man humbleth himself not, therefore, forgive him not.

10. O ye wicked ones, enter into the rock, and hide thee in the dust, for the fear of the Lord and the glory of his majesty shall smite thee.

11. And it shall come to pass that the lofty looks of man shall be humbled, and the haughtiness of men shall be bowed down, and the Lord alone shall be exalted in that day.

12. For the day of the Lord of Hosts soon cometh upon all nations, yea, upon every one; yea, upon the proud and lofty, and upon every one who is lifted up, and he shall be brought low.

13. Yea, and the day of the Lord shall come upon all the cedars of Lebanon, for they are high and lifted up; and upon all the oaks of Bashan;

14. And upon all the high mountains, and upon all the hills, and upon all the nations which are lifted up, and upon every people;

15. And upon every high tower, and upon every fenced wall;

16. And upon all the ships of the sea, and upon all the ships of Tarshish, and upon all pleasant pictures.

17. And the loftiness of man shall be bowed down, and the haughtiness of men shall be made low; and the Lord alone shall be exalted in that day.

18. And the idols he shall utterly abolish.

19. And they shall go into the holes of the rocks, and into the caves of the earth, for the fear of the Lord shall come upon them and the glory of his majesty shall smite them, when he ariseth to shake terribly the earth.

20. In that day a man shall cast his idols of silver,

and his idols of gold, which he hath made for himself to worship, to the moles and to the bats;

21. To go into the clefts of the rocks, and into the tops of the ragged rocks, for the fear of the Lord shall come upon them and the majesty of his glory shall smite them, when he ariseth to shake terribly the earth.

22. Cease ye from man, whose breath is in his nostrils; for wherein is he to be accounted of?

CHAPTER 13.

1. For behold, the Lord, the Lord of Hosts, doth take away from Jerusalem, and from Judah, the stay and the staff, the whole staff of bread, and the whole stay of water—

2. The mighty man, and the man of war, the judge, and the prophet, and the prudent, and the ancient;

3. The captain of fifty, and the honorable man, and the counselor, and the cunning artificer, and the eloquent orator.

4. And I will give children unto them to be their princes, and babes shall rule over them.

5. And the people shall be oppressed, every one by another, and every one by his neighbor; the child shall behave himself proudly against the ancient, and the base against the honorable.

6. When a man shall take hold of his brother of the house of his father, and shall say: Thou hast clothing, be thou our ruler, and let not this ruin come under thy hand—

7. In that day shall he swear, saying: I will not be a healer; for in my house there is neither bread nor clothing; make me not a ruler of the people.

8. For Jerusalem is ruined, and Judah is fallen, because their tongues and their doings have been against the Lord, to provoke the eyes of his glory.

9. The show of their countenance doth witness against them, and doth declare their sin to be even as Sodom, and they cannot hide it. Wo unto their souls, for they have rewarded evil unto themselves!

10. Say unto the righteous that it is well with them; for they shall eat the fruit of their doings.

11. Wo unto the wicked, for they shall perish; for the reward of their hands shall be upon them!

12. And my people, children are their oppressors, and women rule over them. O my people, they who lead thee cause thee to err and destroy the way of thy paths.

13. The Lord standeth up to plead, and standeth to judge the people.

14. The Lord will enter into judgment with the ancients of his people and the princes thereof; for ye have eaten up the vineyard and the spoil of the poor in your houses.

15. What mean ye? Ye beat my people to pieces, and grind the faces of the poor, saith the Lord God of Hosts.

16. Moreover, the Lord saith: Because the daughters of Zion are haughty, and walk with stretched-forth necks and wanton eyes, walking and mincing as they go, and making a tinkling with their feet—

17. Therefore the Lord will smite with a scab the crown of the head of the daughters of Zion, and the Lord will discover their secret parts.

18. In that day the Lord will take away the bravery of their tinkling ornaments, and cauls, and round tires like the moon;

19. The chains and the bracelets, and the mufflers;

20. The bonnets, and the ornaments of the legs, and the headbands, and the tablets, and the ear-rings;

21. The rings, and nose jewels;

22. The changeable suits of apparel, and the mantles, and the wimples, and the crisping-pins;

23. The glasses, and the fine linen, and hoods, and the veils.

24. And it shall come to pass, instead of sweet smell there shall be stink; and instead of a girdle, a rent; and instead of well set hair, baldness; and instead of a stomacher, a girding of sackcloth; burning instead of beauty.

25. Thy men shall fall by the sword and thy mighty in the war.

26. And her gates shall lament and mourn; and she shall be desolate, and shall sit upon the ground.

CHAPTER 14.

1. And in that day, seven women shall take hold of one man, saying: We will eat our own bread, and wear our own apparel; only let us be called by thy name to take away our reproach.

2. In that day shall the branch of the Lord be beautiful and glorious; the fruit of the earth excellent and comely to them that are escaped of Israel.

3. And it shall come to pass, they that are left in Zion and remain in Jerusalem shall be called holy, every one that is written among the living in Jerusalem—

4. When the Lord shall have washed away the filth of the daughters of Zion, and shall have purged the blood of Jerusalem from the midst thereof by the spirit of judgment and by the spirit of burning.

5. And the Lord will create upon every dwelling-place of mount Zion, and upon her assemblies, a cloud and

smoke by day and the shining of a flaming fire by night; for upon all the glory of Zion shall be a defence.

6.   And there shall be a tabernacle for a shadow in the daytime from the heat, and for a place of refuge, and a covert from storm and from rain.

CHAPTER 15.

1.   And then will I sing to my well-beloved a song of my beloved, touching his vineyard. My well-beloved hath a vineyard in a very fruitful hill.

2.   And he fenced it, and gathered out the stones thereof, and planted it with the choicest vine, and built a tower in the midst of it, and also made a wine-press therein; and he looked that it should bring forth grapes, and it brought forth wild grapes.

3.   And now, O inhabitants of Jerusalem, and men of Judah, judge, I pray you, betwixt me and my vineyard.

4.   What could have been done more to my vineyard that I have not done in it? Wherefore, when I looked that it should bring forth grapes it brought forth wild grapes.

5.   And now go to; I will tell you what I will do to my vineyard—I will take away the hedge thereof, and it shall be eaten up; and I will break down the wall thereof, and it shall be trodden down;

6.   And I will lay it waste; it shall not be pruned nor digged; but there shall come up briers and thorns; I will also command the clouds that they rain no rain upon it.

7.   For the vineyard of the Lord of Hosts is the house of Israel, and the men of Judah his pleasant plant; and he looked for judgment, and behold, oppression; for righteousness, but behold, a cry.

8.   Wo unto them that join house to house, till there can be no place, that they may be placed alone in the midst of the earth!

9.   In mine ears, said the Lord of Hosts, of a truth many houses shall be desolate, and great and fair cities without inhabitant.

10.   Yea, ten acres of vineyard shall yield one bath, and the seed of a homer shall yield an ephah.

11.   Wo unto them that rise up early in the morning, that they may follow strong drink, that continue until night, and wine inflame them!

12.   And the harp, and the viol, the tabret, and pipe, and wine are in their feasts; but they regard not the work of the Lord, neither consider the operation of his hands.

13.   Therefore, my people are gone into captivity, because they have no knowledge; and their honorable men are famished, and their multitude dried up with thirst.

14.   Therefore, hell hath enlarged herself, and opened her mouth without measure; and their glory, and their multitude, and their pomp, and he that rejoiceth, shall descend into it.

15.   And the mean man shall be brought down, and the mighty man shall be humbled, and the eyes of the lofty shall be humbled.

16.   But the Lord of Hosts shall be exalted in judgment, and God that is holy shall be sanctified in righteousness.

17.   Then shall the lambs feed after their manner, and the waste places of the fat ones shall strangers eat.

18.   Wo unto them that draw iniquity with cords of vanity, and sin as it were with a cart rope;

19.   That say: Let him make speed, hasten his work, that we may see it; and let the counsel of the Holy One of Israel draw nigh and come, that we may know it.

20.   Wo unto them that call evil good, and good evil, that put darkness for light, and light for darkness, that put bitter for sweet, and sweet for bitter!

21.   Wo unto the wise in their own eyes and prudent in their own sight!

22.   Wo unto the mighty to drink wine, and men of strength to mingle strong drink;

23.   Who justify the wicked for reward, and take away the righteousness of the righteous from him!

24.   Therefore, as the fire devoureth the stubble, and the flame consumeth the chaff, their root shall be rottenness, and their blossoms shall go up as dust; because they have cast away the law of the Lord of Hosts, and despised the word of the Holy One of Israel.

25.   Therefore, is the anger of the Lord kindled against his people, and he hath stretched forth his hand against them, and hath smitten them; and the hills did tremble, and their carcasses were torn in the midst of the streets. For all this his anger is not turned away, but his hand is stretched out still.

26.   And he will lift up an ensign to the nations from far, and will hiss unto them from the end of the earth; and behold, they shall come with speed swiftly; none shall be weary nor stumble among them.

27.   None shall slumber nor sleep; neither shall the girdle of their loins be loosed, nor the latchet of their shoes be broken;

28.   Whose arrows shall be sharp, and all their bows bent, and their horses' hoofs shall be counted like flint, and their wheels like a whirlwind, their roaring like a lion.

29.   They shall roar like young lions; yea, they shall roar, and lay hold of the prey, and shall carry away safe, and none shall deliver.

30.   And in that day they shall roar against them like the roaring of the sea; and if they look unto the land, behold, darkness and sorrow, and the light is darkened in the heavens thereof.

CHAPTER 16.

1. In the year that king Uzziah died, I saw also the Lord sitting upon a throne, high and lifted up, and his train filled the temple.

2. Above it stood the seraphim; each one had six wings; with twain he covered his face, and with twain he covered his feet, and with twain he did fly.

3. And one cried unto another, and said: Holy, holy, holy, is the Lord of Hosts; the whole earth is full of his glory.

4. And the posts of the door moved at the voice of him that cried, and the house was filled with smoke.

5. Then said I: Wo is unto me! for I am undone; because I am a man of unclean lips; and I dwell in the midst of a people of unclean lips; for mine eyes have seen the King, the Lord of Hosts.

6. Then flew one of the seraphim unto me, having a live coal in his hand, which he had taken with the tongs from off the altar;

7. And he laid it upon my mouth, and said: Lo, this has touched thy lips; and thine iniquity is taken away, and thy sin purged.

8. Also I heard the voice of the Lord, saying: Whom shall I send, and who will go for us? Then I said: Here am I; send me.

9. And he said: Go and tell this people—Hear ye indeed, but they understood not; and see ye indeed, but they perceived not.

10. Make the heart of this people fat, and make their ears heavy, and shut their eyes—lest they see with their eyes, and hear with their ears, and understand with their heart, and be converted and be healed.

11. Then said I: Lord, how long? And he said: Until the cities be wasted without inhabitant, and the houses without man, and the land be utterly desolate;

12. And the Lord have removed men far away, for there shall be a great forsaking in the midst of the land.

13. But yet there shall be a tenth, and they shall return, and shall be eaten, as a teil-tree, and as an oak whose substance is in them when they cast their leaves; so the holy seed shall be the substance thereof.

CHAPTER 17.

1. And it came to pass in the days of Ahaz the son of Jotham, the son of Uzziah, king of Judah, that Rezin, king of Syria, and Pekah the son of Remaliah, king of Israel, went up toward Jerusalem to war against it, but could not prevail against it.

2. And it was told the house of David, saying: Syria is confederate with Ephraim. And his heart was moved, and the heart of his people, as the trees of the wood are moved with the wind.

3. Then said the Lord unto Isaiah: Go forth now to meet Ahaz, thou and Shearjashub thy son, at the end of the conduit of the upper pool in the highway of the fuller's field;

4. And say unto him: Take heed, and be quiet; fear not, neither be faint-hearted for the two tails of these smoking firebrands, for the fierce anger of Rezin with Syria, and of the son of Remaliah.

5. Because Syria, Ephraim, and the son of Remaliah, have taken evil counsel against thee, saying:

6. Let us go up against Judah and vex it, and let us make a breach therein for us, and set a king in the midst of it, yea, the son of Tabeal.

7. Thus saith the Lord God: It shall not stand, neither shall it come to pass.

8. For the head of Syria is Damascus, and the head of Damascus, Rezin; and within three score and five years shall Ephraim be broken that it be not a people.

9. And the head of Ephraim is Samaria, and the head of Samaria is Remaliah's son. If ye will not believe surely ye shall not be established.

10. Moreover, the Lord spake again unto Ahaz, saying:

11. Ask thee a sign of the Lord thy God; ask it either in the depths, or in the heights above.

12. But Ahaz said: I will not ask, neither will I tempt the Lord.

13. And he said: Hear ye now, O house of David; is it a small thing for you to weary men, but will ye weary my God also?

14. Therefore, the Lord himself shall give you a sign—Behold, a virgin shall conceive, and shall bear a son, and shall call his name Immanuel.

15. Butter and honey shall he eat, that he may know to refuse the evil and to choose the good.

16. For before the child shall know to refuse the evil and choose the good, the land that thou abhorrest shall be forsaken of both her kings.

17. The Lord shall bring upon thee, and upon thy people, and upon thy father's house, days that have not come from the day that Ephraim departed from Judah, the king of Assyria.

18. And it shall come to pass in that day that the Lord shall hiss for the fly that is in the uttermost part of Egypt, and for the bee that is in the land of Assyria.

19. And they shall come, and shall rest all of them in the desolate valleys, and in the holes of the rocks, and upon all thorns, and upon all bushes.

20. In the same day shall the Lord shave with a razor that is hired, by them beyond the river, by the king of Assyria, the head, and the hair of the feet; and it shall also consume the beard.

21. And it shall come to pass in that day, a man shall nourish a young cow and two sheep;

22. And it shall come to pass, for the abundance of milk they shall give he shall eat butter; for butter and honey shall every one eat that is left in the land.

23. And it shall come to pass in that day, every place shall be, where there were a thousand vines at a thousand silverlings, which shall be for briers and thorns.

24. With arrows and with bows shall men come thither, because all the land shall become briers and thorns.

25. And all hills that shall be digged with the mattock, there shall not come thither the fear of briers and thorns; but it shall be for the sending forth of oxen, and the treading of lesser cattle.

CHAPTER 18.

1. Moreover, the word of the Lord said unto me: Take thee a great roll, and write in it with a man's pen, concerning Maher-shalal-hash-baz.

2. And I took unto me faithful witnesses to record, Uriah the priest, and Zechariah the son of Jeberechiah.

3. And I went unto the prophetess; and she conceived and bare a son. Then said the Lord to me: Call his name, Maher-shalal-hash-baz.

4. For behold, the child shall not have knowledge to cry, My father, and my mother, before the riches of Damascus and the spoil of Samaria shall be taken away before the king of Assyria.

5. The Lord spake also unto me again, saying:

6. Forasmuch as this people refuseth the waters of Shiloah that go softly, and rejoice in Rezin and Remaliah's son;

7. Now therefore, behold, the Lord bringeth up upon them the waters of the river, strong and many, even the king of Assyria and all his glory; and he shall come up over all his channels, and go over all his banks.

8. And he shall pass through Judah; he shall overflow and go over, he shall reach even to the neck; and the stretching out of his wings shall fill the breadth of thy land, O Immanuel.

9. Associate yourselves, O ye people, and ye shall be broken in pieces; and give ear all ye of far countries; gird yourselves, and ye shall be broken in pieces; gird yourselves, and ye shall be broken in pieces.

10. Take counsel together, and it shall come to naught; speak the word, and it shall not stand; for God is with us.

11. For the Lord spake thus to me with a strong hand, and instructed me that I should not walk in the way of this people, saying:

12. Say ye not, A confederacy, to all to whom this people shall say, A confederacy; neither fear ye their fear, nor be afraid.

13. Sanctify the Lord of Hosts himself, and let him be your fear, and let him be your dread.

14. And he shall be for a sanctuary; but for a stone of stumbling, and for a rock of offense to both the houses of Israel, for a gin and a snare to the inhabitants of Jerusalem.

15. And many among them shall stumble and fall, and be broken, and be snared, and be taken.

16. Bind up the testimony, seal the law among my disciples.

17. And I will wait upon the Lord, that hideth his face from the house of Jacob, and I will look for him.

18. Behold, I and the children whom the Lord hath given me are for signs and for wonders in Israel from the Lord of Hosts, which dwelleth in Mount Zion.

19. And when they shall say unto you: Seek unto them that have familiar spirits, and unto wizards that peep and mutter—should not a people seek unto their God for the living to hear from the dead?

20. To the law and to the testimony; and if they speak not according to this word, it is because there is no light in them.

21. And they shall pass through it hardly bestead and hungry; and it shall come to pass that when they shall be hungry, they shall fret themselves, and curse their king and their God, and look upward.

22. And they shall look unto the earth and behold trouble, and darkness, dimness of anguish, and shall be driven to darkness.

CHAPTER 19.

1. Nevertheless, the dimness shall not be such as was in her vexation, when at first he lightly afflicted the land of Zebulun, and the land of Naphtali, and afterwards did more grievously afflict by the way of the Red Sea beyond Jordan in Galilee of the nations.

2. The people that walked in darkness have seen a great light; they that dwell in the land of the shadow of death, upon them hath the light shined.

3. Thou hast multiplied the nation, and increased the joy—they joy before thee according to the joy in harvest, and as men rejoice when they divide the spoil.

4. For thou hast broken the yoke of his burden, and the staff of his shoulder, the rod of his oppressor.

5. For every battle of the warrior is with confused noise, and garments rolled in blood; but this shall be with burning and fuel of fire.

6. For unto us a child is born, unto us a son is given; and the government shall be upon his shoulder; and his name shall be called, Wonderful, Counselor, The Mighty God, The Everlasting Father, The Prince of Peace.

7. Of the increase of government and peace there is no end, upon the throne of David, and upon his kingdom to order it, and to establish it with judgment and with justice from henceforth, even forever. The zeal of the Lord of Hosts will perform this.

8. The Lord sent his word unto Jacob and it hath lighted upon Israel.

9. And all the people shall know, even Ephraim and the inhabitants of Samaria, that say in the pride and stoutness of heart:

10. The bricks are fallen down, but we will build with hewn stones; the sycamores are cut down, but we will change them into cedars.

11. Therefore the Lord shall set up the adversaries of Rezin against him, and join his enemies together;

12. The Syrians before and the Philistines behind; and they shall devour Israel with open mouth. For all this his anger is not turned away, but his hand is stretched out still.

13. For the people turneth not unto him that smiteth them, neither do they seek the Lord of Hosts.

14. Therefore will the Lord cut off from Israel head and tail, branch and rush in one day.

15. The ancient, he is the head; and the prophet that teacheth lies, he is the tail.

16. For the leaders of this people cause them to err; and they that are led of them are destroyed.

17. Therefore the Lord shall have no joy in their young men, neither shall have mercy on their fatherless and widows; for every one of them is a hypocrite and an evildoer, and every mouth speaketh folly. For all this his anger is not turned away, but his hand is stretched out still.

18. For wickedness burneth as the fire; it shall devour the briers and thorns, and shall kindle in the thickets of the forests, and they shall mount up like the lifting up of smoke.

19. Through the wrath of the Lord of Hosts is the land darkened, and the people shall be as the fuel of the fire; no man shall spare his brother.

20. And he shall snatch on the right hand and be hungry; and he shall eat on the left hand and they shall not be satisfied; they shall eat every man the flesh of his own arm—

21. Manasseh, Ephraim; and Ephraim, Manasseh; they together shall be against Judah. For all this his anger is not turned away, but his hand is stretched out still.

CHAPTER 20.

1. Wo unto them that decree unrighteous decrees, and that write grievousness which they have prescribed;

2. To turn away the needy from judgment, and to take away the right from the poor of my people, that widows may be their prey, and that they may rob the fatherless!

3. And what will ye do in the day of visitation, and in the desolation which shall come from far? to whom will ye flee for help? and where will ye leave your glory?

4. Without me they shall bow down under the prisoners, and they shall fall under the slain. For all this his anger is not turned away, but his hand is stretched out still.

5. O Assyrian, the rod of mine anger, and the staff in their hand is their indignation.

6. I will send him against a hypocritical nation, and against the people of my wrath will I give him a charge to take the spoil, and to take the prey, and to tread them down like the mire of the streets.

7. Howbeit he meaneth not so, neither doth his heart think so; but in his heart it is to destroy and cut off nations not a few.

8. For he saith: Are not my princes altogether kings?

9. Is not Calno as Carchemish? Is not Hamath as Arpad? Is not Samaria as Damascus?

10. As my hand hath founded the kingdoms of the idols, and whose graven images did excel them of Jerusalem and of Samaria;

11. Shall I not, as I have done unto Samaria and her idols, so do to Jerusalem and to her idols?

12. Wherefore it shall come to pass that when the Lord hath performed his whole work upon Mount Zion and upon Jerusalem, I will punish the fruit of the stout heart of the king of Assyria, and the glory of his high looks.

13. For he saith: By the strength of my hand and by my wisdom I have done these things; for I am prudent; and I have moved the borders of the people, and have robbed their treasures, and I have put down the inhabitants like a valiant man;

14. And my hand hath found as a nest the riches of the people; and as one gathereth eggs that are left have I gathered all the earth; and there was none that moved the wing, or opened the mouth, or peeped.

15. Shall the ax boast itself against him that heweth therewith? Shall the saw magnify itself against him that shaketh it? As if the rod should shake itself against them that lift it up, or as if the staff should lift up itself as if it were no wood!

16. Therefore shall the Lord, the Lord of Hosts, send among his fat ones, leanness; and under his glory he shall kindle a burning like the burning of a fire.

17. And the light of Israel shall be for a fire, and his Holy One for a flame, and shall burn and shall devour his thorns and his briers in one day;

18. And shall consume the glory of his forest, and of his fruitful field, both soul and body; and they shall be as when a standard-bearer fainteth.

19. And the rest of the trees of his forest shall be few, that a child may write them.

20. And it shall come to pass in that day, that the remnant of Israel, and such as are escaped of the house of Jacob, shall no more again stay upon him that smote them, but shall stay upon the Lord, the Holy One of Israel, in truth.

21. The remnant shall return, yea, even the remnant of Jacob, unto the mighty God.

22. For though thy people Israel be as the sand of the sea, yet a remnant of them shall return; the consumption decreed shall overflow with righteousness.

23. For the Lord God of Hosts shall make a consumption, even determined in all the land.

24. Therefore, thus saith the Lord God of Hosts; O my people that dwellest in Zion, be not afraid of the Assyrian; he shall smite thee with a rod, and shall lift up his staff against thee, after the manner of Egypt.

25. For yet a very little while, and the indignation shall cease, and mine anger in their destruction.

26. And the Lord of Hosts shall stir up a scourge for him according to the slaughter of Midian at the rock of Oreb; and as his rod was upon the sea so shall he lift it up after the manner of Egypt.

27. And it shall come to pass in that day that his burden shall be taken away from off thy shoulder, and his yoke from off thy neck, and the yoke shall be destroyed because of the anointing.

28. He is come to Aiath, he is passed to Migron; at Michmash he hath laid up his carriages.

29. They are gone over the passage; they have taken up their lodging at Geba; Ramath is afraid; Gibeah of Saul is fled.

30. Lift up the voice, O daughter of Gallim; cause it to be heard unto Laish, O poor Anathoth.

31. Madmenah is removed; the inhabitants of Gebim gather themselves to flee.

32. As yet shall he remain at Nob that day; he shall shake his hand against the mount of the daughter of Zion, the hill of Jerusalem.

33. Behold, the Lord, the Lord of Hosts shall lop the bough with terror; and the high ones of stature shall be hewn down; and the haughty shall be humbled.

34. And he shall cut down the thickets of the forests with iron, and Lebanon shall fall by a mighty one.

CHAPTER 21.

1. And there shall come forth a rod out of the stem of Jesse, and a branch shall grow out of his roots.

2. And the Spirit of the Lord shall rest upon him, the spirit of wisdom and understanding, the spirit of counsel and might, the spirit of knowledge and of the fear of the Lord;

3. And shall make him of quick understanding in the fear of the Lord; and he shall not judge after the sight of his eyes, neither reprove after the hearing of his ears.

4. But with righteousness shall he judge the poor, and reprove with equity for the meek of the earth; and he shall smite the earth with the rod of his mouth, and with the breath of his lips shall he slay the wicked.

5. And righteousness shall be the girdle of his loins, and faithfulness the girdle of his reins.

6. The wolf also shall dwell with the lamb, and the leopard shall lie down with the kid, and the calf and the young lion and fatling together; and a little child shall lead them.

7. And the cow and the bear shall feed; their young ones shall lie down together; and the lion shall eat straw like the ox.

8. And the sucking child shall play on the hole of the asp, and the weaned child shall put his hand on the cockatrice's den.

9. They shall not hurt nor destroy in all my holy mountain, for the earth shall be full of the knowledge of the Lord, as the waters cover the sea.

10. And in that day there shall be a root of Jesse, which shall stand for an ensign of the people; to it shall the Gentiles seek; and his rest shall be glorious.

11. And it shall come to pass in that day that the Lord shall set his hand again the second time to recover the remnant of his people which shall be left, from Assyria,

and from Egypt, and from Pathros, and from Cush, and from Elam, and from Shinar, and from Hamath, and from the islands of the sea.

12. And he shall set up an ensign for the nations, and shall assemble the outcasts of Israel, and gather together the dispersed of Judah from the four corners of the earth.

13. The envy of Ephraim also shall depart, and the adversaries of Judah shall be cut off; Ephraim shall not envy Judah, and Judah shall not vex Ephraim.

14. But they shall fly upon the shoulders of the Philistines towards the west; they shall spoil them of the east together; they shall lay their hand upon Edom and Moab; and the children of Ammon shall obey them.

15. And the Lord shall utterly destroy the tongue of the Egyptian sea; and with his mighty wind he shall shake his hand over the river, and shall smite it in the seven streams, and make men go over dry shod.

16. And there shall be a highway for the remnant of his people which shall be left, from Assyria, like as it was to Israel in the day that he came up out of the land of Egypt.

CHAPTER 22

1. And in that day thou shalt say: O Lord, I will praise thee; though thou wast angry with me thine anger is turned away, and thou comfortedst me.

2. Behold, God is my salvation; I will trust, and not be afraid; for the Lord JEHOVAH is my strength and my song; he also has become my salvation.

3. Therefore, with joy shall ye draw water out of the wells of salvation.

4. And in that day shall ye say: Praise the Lord, call upon his name, declare his doings among the people, make mention that his name is exalted.

5. Sing unto the Lord; for he hath done excellent things; this is known in all the earth.

6. Cry out and shout, thou inhabitant of Zion; for great is the Holy One of Israel in the midst of thee.

CHAPTER 23.

1. The burden of Babylon, which Isaiah the son of Amoz did see.

2. Lift ye up a banner upon the high mountain, exalt the voice unto them, shake the hand, that they may go into the gates of the nobles.

3. I have commanded my sanctified ones, I have also called my mighty ones, for mine anger is not upon them that rejoice in my highness.

4. The noise of the multitude in the mountains like as of a great people, a tumultuous noise of the kingdoms of nations gathered together, the Lord of Hosts mustereth the hosts of the battle.

5. They come from a far country, from the end of heaven, yea, the Lord, and the weapons of his indignation, to destroy the whole land.

6. Howl ye, for the day of the Lord is at hand; it shall come as a destruction from the Almighty.

7. Therefore shall all hands be faint, every man's heart shall melt;

8. And they shall be afraid; pangs and sorrows shall take hold of them; they shall be amazed one at another; their faces shall be as flames.

9. Behold, the day of the Lord cometh, cruel both with wrath and fierce anger, to lay the land desolate; and he shall destroy the sinners thereof out of it.

10. For the stars of heaven and the constellations thereof shall not give their light; the sun shall be darkened in her going forth, and the moon shall not cause her light to shine.

11. And I will punish the world for evil, and the wicked for their iniquity; I will cause the arrogancy of the proud to cease, and will lay down the haughtiness of the terrible.

12. I will make a man more precious than fine gold; even a man than the golden wedge of Ophir.

13. Therefore, I will shake the heavens, and the earth shall remove out of her place, in the wrath of the Lord of Hosts, and in the day of his fierce anger.

14. And it shall be as the chased roe, and as a sheep that no man taketh up; and they shall every man turn to his own people, and flee every one into his own land.

15. Every one that is proud shall be thrust through; yea, and every one that is joined to the wicked shall fall by the sword.

16. Their children also shall be dashed to pieces before their eyes; their houses shall be spoiled and their wives ravished.

17. Behold, I will stir up the Medes against them, which shall not regard silver and gold, nor shall they delight in it.

18. Their bows shall also dash the young men to pieces, and they shall have no pity on the fruit of the womb; their eyes shall not spare children.

19. And Babylon, the glory of kingdoms, the beauty of the Chaldees' excellency, shall be as when God overthrew Sodom and Gomorrah.

20. It shall never be inhabited, neither shall it be dwelt in from generation to generation: neither shall the Arabian pitch tent there; neither shall the shepherds make their fold there.

21. But wild beasts of the desert shall lie there; and their houses shall be full of doleful creatures; and owls shall dwell there, and satyrs shall dance there.

22. And the wild beasts of the islands shall cry in their desolate houses, and dragons in their pleasant palaces; and her time is near to come, and her day shall not be prolonged. For I will destroy her speedily; yea, for I will be merciful unto my people, but the wicked shall perish.

CHAPTER 24.

1. For the Lord will have mercy on Jacob, and will yet choose Israel, and set them in their own land; and the strangers shall be joined with them, and they shall cleave to the house of Jacob.

2. And the people shall take them and bring them to their place; yea, from far unto the ends of the earth; and they shall return to their lands of promise. And the house of Israel shall possess them, and the land of the Lord shall be for servants and handmaids; and they shall take them captives unto whom they were captives; and they shall rule over their oppressors.

3. And it shall come to pass in that day that the Lord shall give thee rest, from thy sorrow, and from thy fear, and from the hard bondage wherein thou wast made to serve.

4. And it shall come to pass in that day, that thou shalt take up this proverb against the king of Babylon, and say: How hath the oppressor ceased, the golden city ceased!

5. The Lord hath broken the staff of the wicked, the scepters of the rulers.

6. He who smote the people in wrath with a continual stroke, he that ruled the nations in anger, is persecuted, and none hindereth.

7. The whole earth is at rest, and is quiet; they break forth into singing.

8. Yea, the fir-trees rejoice at thee, and also the cedars of Lebanon, saying: Since thou art laid down no feller is come up against us.

9. Hell from beneath is moved for thee to meet thee at thy coming; it stirreth up the dead for thee, even all the chief ones of the earth; it hath raised up from their thrones all the kings of the nations.

10. All they shall speak and say unto thee: Art thou also become weak as we? Art thou become like unto us?

11. Thy pomp is brought down to the grave; the noise of thy viols is not heard; the worm is spread under thee, and the worms cover thee.

12. How art thou fallen from heaven, O Lucifer, son of the morning! Art thou cut down to the ground, which did weaken the nations!

13. For thou hast said in thy heart: I will ascend into heaven, I will exalt my throne above the stars of God; I will sit also upon the mount of the congregation, in the sides of the north;

14. I will ascend above the heights of the clouds; I will be like the Most High.

15. Yet thou shalt be brought down to hell, to the sides of the pit.

16. They that see thee shall narrowly look upon thee, and shall consider thee, and shall say: Is this the man that made the earth to tremble, that did shake kingdoms?

17. And made the world as a wilderness, and destroyed the cities thereof, and opened not the house of his prisoners?

18. All the kings of the nations, yea, all of them, lie in glory, every one of them in his own house.

19. But thou art cast out of thy grave like an abominable branch, and the remnant of those that are slain, thrust through with a sword, that go down to the stones of the pit; as a carcass trodden under feet.

20. Thou shalt not be joined with them in burial, because thou hast destroyed thy land and slain thy people; the seed of evildoers shall never be renowned.

21. Prepare slaughter for his children for the iniquities of their fathers, that they do not rise, nor possess the land, nor fill the face of the world with cities.

22. For I will rise up against them, saith the Lord of Hosts, and cut off from Babylon the name, and remnant, and son, and nephew, saith the Lord.

23. I will also make it a possession for the bittern, and pools of water; and I will sweep it with the besom of destruction, saith the Lord of Hosts.

24. The Lord of Hosts hath sworn, saying: Surely as I have thought, so shall it come to pass; and as I have purposed, so shall it stand—

25. That I will bring the Assyrian in my land, and upon my mountains tread him under foot; then shall his yoke depart from off them, and his burden depart from off their shoulders.

26. This is the purpose that is purposed upon the whole earth; and this is the hand that is stretched out upon all nations.

27. For the Lord of Hosts hath purposed, and who shall disannul? And his hand is stretched out, and who shall turn it back?

28. In the year that king Ahaz died was this burden.

29. Rejoice not thou, whole Palestina, because the rod of him that smote thee is broken; for out of the serpent's root shall come forth a cockatrice, and his fruit shall be

a fiery flying serpent.

30. And the first-born of the poor shall feed, and the needy shall lie down in safety; and I will kill thy root with famine, and he shall slay thy remnant.

31. Howl, O gate; cry, O city; thou, whole Palestina, art dissolved; for there shall come from the north a smoke, and none shall be alone in his appointed times.

32. What shall then answer the messengers of the nations? That the Lord hath founded Zion, and the poor of his people shall trust in it.

CHAPTER 25.

1. Now I, Nephi, do speak somewhat concerning the words which I have written, which have been spoken by the mouth of Isaiah. For behold, Isaiah spake many things which were hard for many of my people to understand; for they know not concerning the manner of prophesying among the Jews.

2. For I, Nephi, have not taught them many things concerning the manner of the Jews; for their works were works of darkness, and their doings were doings of abominations.

3. Wherefore, I write unto my people, unto all those that shall receive hereafter these things which I write, that they may know the judgments of God, that they come upon all nations, according to the word which he hath spoken.

4. Wherefore, hearken, O my people, which are of the house of Israel, and give ear unto my words; for because the words of Isaiah are not plain unto you, nevertheless they are plain unto all those that are filled with the spirit of prophecy. But I give unto you a prophecy, according to the spirit which is in me; wherefore I shall prophesy according to the plainness which hath been with me from the time that I came out from Jerusalem with my father; for behold, my soul delighteth in plainness unto my people, that they may learn.

5. Yea, and my soul delighteth in the words of Isaiah, for I came out from Jerusalem, and mine eyes hath beheld the things of the Jews, and I know that the Jews do understand the things of the prophets, and there is none other people that understand the things which were spoken unto the Jews like unto them, save it be that they are taught after the manner of the things of the Jews.

6. But behold, I, Nephi, have not taught my children after the manner of the Jews; but behold, I, of myself, have dwelt at Jerusalem, wherefore I know concerning the regions round about; and I have made mention unto my children concerning the judgments of God, which hath come to pass among the Jews, unto my children, according to all that which Isaiah hath spoken, and I do not write them.

7. But behold, I proceed with mine own prophecy, according to my plainness; in the which I know that no man can err; nevertheless, in the days that the prophecies of Isaiah shall be fulfilled men shall know of a surety, at the times when they shall come to pass.

8. Wherefore, they are of worth unto the children of men, and he that supposeth that they are not, unto them will I speak particularly, and confine the words unto mine own people; for I know that they shall be of great worth unto them in the last days; for in that day shall they understand them; wherefore, for their good have I written them.

9. And as one generation hath been destroyed among the Jews because of iniquity, even so have they been destroyed from generation to generation according to their iniquities; and never hath any of them been destroyed save it were foretold them by the prophets of the Lord.

10. Wherefore, it hath been told them concerning the destruction which should come upon them, immediately after my father left Jerusalem; nevertheless, they hardened their hearts; and according to my prophecy they have been destroyed, save it be those which are carried away captive into Babylon.

11. And now this I speak because of the spirit which is in me. And notwithstanding they have been carried away they shall return again, and possess the land of Jerusalem; wherefore, they shall be restored again to the land of their inheritance.

12. But, behold, they shall have wars, and rumors of wars; and when the day cometh that the Only Begotten of the Father, yea, even the Father of heaven and of earth, shall manifest himself unto them in the flesh, behold, they will reject him, because of their iniquities, and the hardness of their hearts, and the stiffness of their necks.

13. Behold, they will crucify him; and after he is laid in a sepulchre for the space of three days he shall rise from the dead, with healing in his wings; and all those who shall believe on his name shall be saved in the kingdom of God. Wherefore, my soul delighteth to prophesy concerning him, for I have seen his day, and my heart doth magnify his holy name.

14. And behold it shall come to pass that after the Messiah hath risen from the dead, and hath manifested himself unto his people, unto as many as will believe on his name, behold, Jerusalem shall be destroyed again; for wo unto them that fight against God and the people of his church.

15. Wherefore, the Jews shall be scattered among

all nations; yea, and also Babylon shall be destroyed; wherefore, the Jews shall be scattered by other nations.

16. And after they have been scattered, and the Lord God hath scourged them by other nations for the space of many generations, yea, even down from generation to generation until they shall be persuaded to believe in Christ, the Son of God, and the atonement, which is infinite for all mankind—and when that day shall come that they shall believe in Christ, and worship the Father in his name, with pure hearts and clean hands, and look not forward any more for another Messiah, then, at that time, the day will come that it must needs be expedient that they should believe these things.

17. And the Lord will set his hand again the second time to restore his people from their lost and fallen state. Wherefore, he will proceed to do a marvelous work and a wonder among the children of men.

18. Wherefore, he shall bring forth his words unto them, which words shall judge them at the last day, for they shall be given them for the purpose of convincing them of the true Messiah, who was rejected by them; and unto the convincing of them that they need not look forward any more for a Messiah to come, for there should not any come, save it should be a false Messiah which should deceive the people; for there is save one Messiah spoken of by the prophets, and that Messiah is he who should be rejected of the Jews.

19. For according to the words of the prophets, the Messiah cometh in six hundred years from the time that my father left Jerusalem; and according to the words of the prophets, and also the word of the angel of God, his name shall be Jesus Christ, the Son of God.

20. And now, my brethren, I have spoken plainly that ye cannot err. And as the Lord God liveth that brought Israel up out of the land of Egypt, and gave unto Moses power that he should heal the nations after they had been bitten by the poisonous serpents, if they would cast their eyes unto the serpent which he did raise up before them, and also gave him power that he should smite the rock and the water should come forth; yea, behold I say unto you, that as these things are true, and as the Lord God liveth, there is none other name given under heaven save it be this Jesus Christ, of which I have spoken, whereby man can be saved.

21. Wherefore, for this cause hath the Lord God promised unto me that these things which I write shall be kept and preserved, and handed down unto my seed,

from generation to generation, that the promise may be fulfilled unto Joseph, that his seed should never perish as long as the earth should stand.

22. Wherefore, these things shall go from generation to generation as long as the earth shall stand; and they shall go according to the will and pleasure of God; and the nations who shall possess them shall be judged of them according to the words which are written.

23. For we labor diligently to write, to persuade our children, and also our brethren, to believe in Christ, and to be reconciled to God; for we know that it is by grace that we are saved, after all we can do.

24. And, notwithstanding we believe in Christ, we keep the law of Moses, and look forward with steadfastness unto Christ, until the law shall be fulfilled.

25. For, for this end was the law given; wherefore the law hath become dead unto us, and we are made alive in Christ because of our faith; yet we keep the law because of the commandments.

26. And we talk of Christ, we rejoice in Christ, we preach of Christ, we prophesy of Christ, and we write according to our prophecies, that our children may know to what source they may look for a remission of their sins.

27. Wherefore, we speak concerning the law that our children may know the deadness of the law; and they, by knowing the deadness of the law, may look forward unto that life which is in Christ, and know for what end the law was given. And after the law is fulfilled in Christ, that they need not harden their hearts against him when the law ought to be done away.

28. And now behold, my people, ye are a stiffnecked people; wherefore, I have spoken plainly unto you, that ye cannot misunderstand. And the words which I have spoken shall stand as a testimony against you; for they are sufficient to teach any man the right way; for the right way is to believe in Christ and deny him not; for by denying him ye also deny the prophets and the law.

29. And now behold, I say unto you that the right way is to believe in Christ, and deny him not; and Christ is the Holy One of Israel; wherefore ye must bow down before him, and worship him with all your might, mind, and strength, and your whole soul; and if ye do this ye shall in nowise be cast out.

30. And, inasmuch as it shall be expedient, ye must keep the performances and ordinances of God until the law shall be fulfilled which was given unto Moses.

CHAPTER 26

1. And after Christ shall have risen from the dead he shall show himself unto you, my children, and my beloved brethren; and the words which he shall speak unto you shall be the law which ye shall do.

2. For behold, I say unto you that I have beheld that many generations shall pass away, and there shall be great wars and contentions among my people.

3. And after the Messiah shall come there shall be signs given unto my people of his birth, and also of his death and resurrection; and great and terrible shall that day be unto the wicked, for they shall perish; and they perish because they cast out the prophets, and the saints, and stone them, and slay them; wherefore the cry of the blood of the saints shall ascend up to God from the ground against them.

4. Wherefore, all those who are proud, and that do wickedly, the day that cometh shall burn them up, saith the Lord of Hosts, for they shall be as stubble.

5. And they that kill the prophets, and the saints, the depths of the earth shall swallow them up, saith the Lord of Hosts; and mountains shall cover them, and whirlwinds shall carry them away, and buildings shall fall upon them and crush them to pieces and grind them to powder.

6. And they shall be visited with thunderings, and lightnings, and earthquakes, and all manner of destructions, for the fire of the anger of the Lord shall be kindled against them, and they shall be as stubble, and the day that cometh shall consume them, saith the Lord of Hosts.

7. O the pain, and the anguish of my soul for the loss of the slain of my people! For I, Nephi, have seen it, and it well nigh consumeth me before the presence of the Lord; but I must cry unto my God: Thy ways are just.

8. But behold, the righteous that hearken unto the words of the prophets, and destroy them not, but look forward unto Christ with steadfastness for the signs which are given, notwithstanding all persecution—behold, they are they which shall not perish.

9. But the Son of righteousness shall appear unto them; and he shall heal them, and they shall have peace with him, until three generations shall have passed away, and many of the fourth generation shall have passed away in righteousness.

10. And when these things have passed away a speedy destruction cometh unto my people; for, notwithstanding the pains of my soul, I have seen it; wherefore, I know that it shall come to pass; and they sell themselves for naught; for, for the reward of their pride and their foolishness they shall reap destruction; for because they yield unto the devil and choose works of darkness rather than light, therefore they must go down to hell.

11. For the Spirit of the Lord will not always strive with man. And when the Spirit ceaseth to strive with man then cometh speedy destruction, and this grieveth my soul.

12. And as I spake concerning the convincing of the Jews, that Jesus is the very Christ, it must needs be that the Gentiles be convinced also that Jesus is the Christ, the Eternal God;

13. And that he manifesteth himself unto all those who believe in him, by the power of the Holy Ghost; yea, unto every nation, kindred, tongue, and people, working mighty miracles, signs, and wonders, among the children of men according to their faith.

14. But behold, I prophesy unto you concerning the last days; concerning the days when the Lord God shall bring these things forth unto the children of men.

15. After my seed and the seed of my brethren shall have dwindled in unbelief, and shall have been smitten by the Gentiles; yea, after the Lord God shall have camped against them round about, and shall have laid siege against them with a mount, and raised forts against them; and after they shall have been brought down low in the dust, even that they are not, yet the words of the righteous shall be written, and the prayers of the faithful shall be heard, and all those who have dwindled in unbelief shall not be forgotten.

16. For those who shall be destroyed shall speak unto them out of the ground, and their speech shall be low out of the dust, and their voice shall be as one that hath a familiar spirit; for the Lord God will give unto him power, that he may whisper concerning them, even as it were out of the ground; and their speech shall whisper out of the dust.

17. For thus saith the Lord God: They shall write the things which shall be done among them, and they shall be written and sealed up in a book, and those who have dwindled in unbelief shall not have them, for they seek to destroy the things of God.

18. Wherefore, as those who have been destroyed have been destroyed speedily; and the multitude of their terrible ones shall be as chaff that passeth away—yea, thus saith the Lord God: It shall be at an instant, suddenly—

19. And it shall come to pass, that those who have dwindled in unbelief shall be smitten by the hand of the Gentiles.

20. And the Gentiles are lifted up in the pride of their eyes, and have stumbled, because of the greatness of their stumbling block, that they have built up many churches; nevertheless, they put down the power and miracles of God, and preach up unto themselves their own wisdom and their own learning, that they may get gain and grind upon the face of the poor.

21. And there are many churches built up which cause envyings, and strifes, and malice.

22. And there are also secret combinations, even as in times of old, according to the combinations of the devil, for he is the foundation of all these things; yea, the foundation of murder, and works of darkness; yea, and he leadeth them by the neck with a flaxen cord, until he bindeth them with his strong cords forever.

23. For behold, my beloved brethren, I say unto you that the Lord God worketh not in darkness.

24. He doeth not anything save it be for the benefit of the world; for he loveth the world, even that he layeth down his own life that he may draw all men unto him. Wherefore, he commandeth none that they shall not partake of his salvation.

25. Behold, doth he cry unto any, saying: Depart from me? Behold, I say unto you, Nay; but he saith: Come unto me all ye ends of the earth, buy milk and honey, without money and without price.

26. Behold, hath he commanded any that they should depart out of the synagogues, or out of the houses of worship? Behold, I say unto you, Nay.

27. Hath he commanded any that they should not partake of his salvation? Behold I say unto you, Nay; but he hath given it free for all men; and he hath commanded his people that they should persuade all men to repentance.

28. Behold, hath the Lord commanded any that they should not partake of his goodness? Behold I say unto you, Nay; but all men are privileged the one like unto the other, and none are forbidden.

29. He commandeth that there shall be no priestcrafts; for, behold, priestcrafts are that men preach and set themselves up for a light unto the world, that they may get gain and praise of the world; but they seek not the welfare of Zion.

30. Behold, the Lord hath forbidden this thing; wherefore, the Lord God hath given a commandment that all men should have charity, which charity is love. And except they should have charity they were nothing. Wherefore, if they should have charity they would not suffer the laborer in Zion to perish.

31. But the laborer in Zion shall labor for Zion; for if they labor for money they shall perish.

32. And again, the Lord God hath commanded that men should not murder; that they should not lie; that they should not steal; that they should not take the name of the Lord their God in vain; that they should not envy; that they should not have malice; that they should not contend one with another; that they should not commit whoredoms; and that they should do none of these things; for whoso doeth them shall perish.

33. For none of these iniquities come of the Lord; for he doeth that which is good among the children of men; and he doeth nothing save it be plain unto the children of men; and he inviteth them all to come unto him and partake of his goodness; and he denieth none that come unto him, black and white, bond and free, male and female; and he remembereth the heathen; and all are alike unto God, both Jew and Gentile.

CHAPTER 27

1. But, behold, in the last days, or in the days of the Gentiles—yea, behold all the nations of the Gentiles and also the Jews, both those who shall come upon this land and those who shall be upon other lands, yea, even upon all the lands of the earth, behold, they will be drunken with iniquity and all manner of abominations—

2. And when that day shall come they shall be visited of the Lord of Hosts, with thunder and with earthquake, and with a great noise, and with storm, and with tempest, and with the flame of devouring fire.

3. And all the nations that fight against Zion, and that distress her, shall be as a dream of a night vision; yea, it shall be unto them, even as unto a hungry man which dreameth, and behold he eateth but he awaketh and his soul is empty; or like unto a thirsty man which dreameth, and behold he drinketh but he awaketh and behold he is faint, and his soul hath appetite; yea, even so shall the multitude of all the nations be that fight against Mount Zion.

4. For behold, all ye that doeth iniquity, stay yourselves and wonder, for ye shall cry out, and cry; yea, ye shall be drunken but not with wine, ye shall stagger but not with strong drink.

5. For behold, the Lord hath poured out upon you the spirit of deep sleep. For behold, ye have closed your eyes, and ye have rejected the prophets; and your rulers, and the seers hath he covered because of your iniquity.

6. And it shall come to pass that the Lord God shall bring forth unto you the words of a book, and they shall be the words of them which have slumbered.

7. And behold the book shall be sealed; and in the book shall be a revelation from God, from the beginning of the world to the ending thereof.

8. Wherefore, because of the things which are sealed up, the things which are sealed shall not be delivered in the day of the wickedness and abominations of the people. Wherefore the book shall be kept from them.

9. But the book shall be delivered unto a man, and he shall deliver the words of the book, which are the words

of those who have slumbered in the dust, and he shall deliver these words unto another;

10. But the words which are sealed he shall not deliver, neither shall he deliver the book. For the book shall be sealed by the power of God, and the revelation which was sealed shall be kept in the book until the own due time of the Lord, that they may come forth; for behold, they reveal all things from the foundation of the world unto the end thereof.

11. And the day cometh that the words of the book which were sealed shall be read upon the house tops; and they shall be read by the power of Christ; and all things shall be revealed unto the children of men which ever have been among the children of men and which ever will be even unto the end of the earth.

12. Wherefore, at that day when the book shall be delivered unto the man of whom I have spoken, the book shall be hid from the eyes of the world, that the eyes of none shall behold it save it be that three witnesses shall behold it, by the power of God, besides him to whom the book shall be delivered; and they shall testify to the truth of the book and the things therein.

13. And there is none other which shall view it, save it be a few according to the will of God, to bear testimony of his word unto the children of men; for the Lord God hath said that the words of the faithful should speak as if it were from the dead.

14. Wherefore, the Lord God will proceed to bring forth the words of the book; and in the mouth of as many witnesses as seemeth him good will he establish his word; and wo be unto him that rejecteth the word of God!

15. But behold, it shall come to pass that the Lord God shall say unto him to whom he shall deliver the book: Take these words which are not sealed and deliver them to another, that he may show them unto the learned, saying: Read this, I pray thee. And the learned shall say: Bring hither the book, and I will read them.

16. And now, because of the glory of the world and to get gain will they say this, and not for the glory of God.

17. And the man shall say: I cannot bring the book, for it is sealed.

18. Then shall the learned say: I cannot read it.

19. Wherefore it shall come to pass, that the Lord God will deliver again the book and the words thereof to him that is not learned; and the man that is not learned shall say: I am not learned.

20. Then shall the Lord God say unto him: The learned shall not read them, for they have rejected them, and I am able to do mine own work; wherefore thou shalt read the words which I shall give unto thee.

21. Touch not the things which are sealed, for I will bring them forth in mine own due time; for I will show unto the children of men that I am able to do mine own work.

22. Wherefore, when thou hast read the words which I have commanded thee, and obtained the witnesses which I have promised unto thee, then shalt thou seal up the book again, and hide it up unto me, that I may preserve the words which thou hast not read, until I shall see fit in mine own wisdom to reveal all things unto the children of men.

23. For behold, I am God; and I am a God of miracles; and I will show unto the world that I am the same yesterday, today, and forever; and I work not among the children of men save it be according to their faith.

24. And again it shall come to pass that the Lord shall say unto him that shall read the words that shall be delivered him:

25. Forasmuch as this people draw near unto me with their mouth, and with their lips do honor me, but have removed their hearts far from me, and their fear towards me is taught by the precepts of men—

26. Therefore, I will proceed to do a marvelous work among this people, yea, a marvelous work and a wonder, for the wisdom of their wise and learned shall perish and the understanding of their prudent shall be hid.

27. And wo unto them that seek deep to hide their counsel from the Lord! And their works are in the dark; and they say: Who seeth us, and who knoweth us? And they also say: Surely, your turning of things upside down shall be esteemed as the potter's clay. But behold, I will show unto them, saith the Lord of Hosts, that I know all their works. For shall the work say of him that made it, he made me not? Or shall the thing framed say of him that framed it, he had no understanding?

28. But behold, saith the Lord of Hosts: I will show unto the children of men that it is yet a very little while and Lebanon shall be turned into a fruitful field; and the fruitful field shall be esteemed as a forest.

29. And in that day shall the deaf hear the words of the book, and the eyes of the blind shall see out of obscurity and out of darkness.

30. And the meek also shall increase, and their joy shall be in the Lord, and the poor among men shall rejoice in the Holy One of Israel.

31. For assuredly as the Lord liveth they shall see that the terrible one is brought to naught, and the scorner is consumed, and all that watch for iniquity are cut off;

32. And they that make a man an offender for a word, and lay a snare for him that reproveth in the gate, and turn aside the just for a thing of naught.

33. Therefore, thus saith the Lord, who redeemed Abraham, concerning the house of Jacob: Jacob shall not now be ashamed, neither shall his face now wax pale.

34. But when he seeth his children, the work of my

hands, in the midst of him, they shall sanctify my name, and sanctify the Holy One of Jacob, and shall fear the God of Israel.

35. They also that erred in spirit shall come to understanding, and they that murmured shall learn doctrine.

CHAPTER 28.

1. And now, behold, my brethren, I have spoken unto you, according as the Spirit hath constrained me; wherefore, I know that they must surely come to pass.

2. The things which shall be written out of the book shall be of great worth unto the children of men, and especially unto our seed, which is a remnant of the house of Israel.

3. For it shall come to pass in that day that the churches which are built up, and not unto the Lord, when the one shall say unto the other: Behold, I, I am the Lord's; and the others shall say: I, I am the Lord's; and thus shall every one say that hath built up churches, and not unto the Lord—

4. And they shall contend one with another; and their priests shall contend one with another, and they shall teach with their learning, and deny the Holy Ghost, which giveth utterance.

5. And they deny the power of God, the Holy One of Israel; and they say unto the people: Hearken unto us, and hear ye our precept; for behold there is no God today, for the Lord and the Redeemer hath done his work, and he hath given his power unto men:

6. Behold, hearken ye unto my precept; if they shall say there is a miracle wrought by the hand of the Lord, believe it not; for this day he is not a God of miracles; he hath done his work.

7. Yea, and there shall be many which shall say: Eat, drink, and be merry, for tomorrow we die; and it shall be well with us.

8. And there shall also be many which shall say: Eat, drink, and be merry; nevertheless, fear God—he will justify in committing a little sin; yea, lie a little, take the advantage of one because of his words, dig a pit for

thy neighbor; there is no harm in this; and do all these things, for tomorrow we die; and if it so be that we are guilty, God will beat us with a few stripes, and at last we shall be saved in the kingdom of God.

9. Yea, and there shall be many which shall teach after this manner, false and vain and foolish doctrines, and shall be puffed up in their hearts, and shall seek deep to hide their counsels from the Lord; and their works shall be in the dark.

10. And the blood of the saints shall cry from the ground against them.

11. Yea, they have all gone out of the way; they have become corrupted.

12. Because of pride, and because of false teachers, and false doctrine, their churches have become corrupted, and their churches are lifted up; because of pride they are puffed up.

13. They rob the poor because of their fine sanctuaries; they rob the poor because of their fine clothing; and they persecute the meek and the poor in heart, because in their pride they are puffed up.

14. They wear stiff necks and high heads; yea, and because of pride, and wickedness, and abominations, and whoredoms, they have all gone astray save it be a few, who are the humble followers of Christ; nevertheless, they are led, that in many instances they do err because they are taught by the precepts of men.

15. O the wise, and the learned, and the rich, that are puffed up in the pride of their hearts, and all those who preach false doctrines, and all those who commit whoredoms, and pervert the right way of the Lord, wo, wo, wo be unto them, saith the Lord God Almighty, for they shall be thrust down to hell!

16. Wo unto them that turn aside the just for a thing of naught and revile against that which is good, and say that is of no worth! For the day shall come that the Lord God will speedily visit the inhabitants of the earth; and in that day that they are fully ripe in iniquity they shall perish.

17. But behold, if the inhabitants of the earth shall repent of their wickedness and abominations they shall not be destroyed, saith the Lord of Hosts.

18. But behold, that great and abominable church, the whore of all the earth, must tumble to the earth, and great must be the fall thereof.

19. For the kingdom of the devil must shake, and they which belong to it must needs be stirred up unto repentance, or the devil will grasp them with his everlasting chains, and they be stirred up to anger, and perish;

20. For behold, at that day shall he rage in the hearts

of the children of men, and stir them up to anger against that which is good.

21. And others will he pacify, and lull them away into carnal security, that they will say: All is well in Zion; yea, Zion prospereth, all is well—and thus the devil cheateth their souls, and leadeth them away carefully down to hell.

22. And behold, others he flattereth away, and telleth them there is no hell; and he saith unto them: I am no devil, for there is none—and thus he whispereth in their ears, until he grasps them with his awful chains, from whence there is no deliverance.

23. Yea, they are grasped with death, and hell; and death, and hell, and the devil, and all that have been seized therewith must stand before the throne of God, and be judged according to their works, from whence they must go into the place prepared for them, even a lake of fire and brimstone, which is endless torment.

24. Therefore, wo be unto him that is at ease in Zion!

25. Wo be unto him that crieth: All is well!

26. Yea, wo be unto him that hearkeneth unto the precepts of men, and denieth the power of God, and the gift of the Holy Ghost!

27. Yea, wo be unto him that saith: We have received, and we need no more!

28. And in fine, wo unto all those who tremble, and are angry because of the truth of God! For behold, he that is built upon the rock receiveth it with gladness; and he that is built upon a sandy foundation trembleth lest he shall fall.

29. Wo be unto him that shall say: We have received the word of God, and we need no more of the word of God, for we have enough!

30. For behold, thus saith the Lord God: I will give unto the children of men line upon line, precept upon precept, here a little and there a little; and blessed are those who hearken unto my precepts, and lend an ear unto my counsel, for they shall learn wisdom; for unto him that receiveth I will give more; and from them that shall say, We have enough, from them shall be taken away even that which they have.

31. Cursed is he that putteth his trust in man, or maketh flesh his arm, or shall hearken unto the precepts of men, save their precepts shall be given by the power of the Holy Ghost.

32. Wo be unto the Gentiles, saith the Lord God of Hosts! For notwithstanding I shall lengthen out mine arm unto them from day to day, they will deny me; nevertheless, I will be merciful unto them, saith the Lord God, if they will repent and come unto me; for mine arm is lengthened out all the day long, saith the Lord God of Hosts.

CHAPTER 29.

1. But behold, there shall be many—at that day when I shall proceed to do a marvelous work among them, that I may remember my covenants which I have made unto the children of men, that I may set my hand again the second time to recover my people, which are of the house of Israel;

2. And also, that I may remember the promises which I have made unto thee, Nephi, and also unto thy father, that I would remember your seed; and that the words of your seed should proceed forth out of my mouth unto your seed; and my words shall hiss forth unto the ends of the earth, for a standard unto my people, which are of the house of Israel;

3. And because my words shall hiss forth—many of the Gentiles shall say: A Bible! A Bible! We have got a Bible, and there cannot be any more Bible.

4. But thus saith the Lord God: O fools, they shall have a Bible; and it shall proceed forth from the Jews, mine ancient covenant people. And what thank they the Jews for the Bible which they receive from them? Yea, what do the Gentiles mean? Do they remember the travels, and the labors, and the pains of the Jews, and their diligence unto me, in bringing forth salvation unto the Gentiles?

5. O ye Gentiles, have ye remembered the Jews, mine ancient covenant people? Nay; but ye have cursed them, and have hated them, and have not sought to recover them. But behold, I will return all these things upon your own heads; for I the Lord have not forgotten my people.

6. Thou fool, that shall say: A Bible, we have got a Bible, and we need no more Bible. Have ye obtained a Bible save it were by the Jews?

7. Know ye not that there are more nations than one? Know ye not that I, the Lord your God, have created all men, and that I remember those who are upon the isles of the sea; and that I rule in the heavens above and in the earth beneath; and I bring forth my word unto the children of men, yea, even upon all the nations of the earth?

8. Wherefore murmur ye, because that ye shall receive more of my word? Know ye not that the testimony of two nations is a witness unto you that I am God, that I remember one nation like unto another? Wherefore, I speak the same words unto one nation like unto another. And when the two nations shall run together the testimony of the two nations shall run together also.

9. And I do this that I may prove unto many that I am the same yesterday, today, and forever; and that I speak forth my words according to mine own pleasure. And because that I have spoken one word ye need not

suppose that I cannot speak another; for my work is not yet finished; neither shall it be until the end of man, neither from that time henceforth and forever.

10. Wherefore, because that ye have a Bible ye need not suppose that it contains all my words; neither need ye suppose that I have not caused more to be written.

11. For I command all men, both in the east and in the west, and in the north, and in the south, and in the islands of the sea, that they shall write the words which I speak unto them; for out of the books which shall be written I will judge the world, every man according to their works, according to that which is written.

12. For behold, I shall speak unto the Jews and they shall write it; and I shall also speak unto the Nephites and they shall write it; and I shall also speak unto the other tribes of the house of Israel, which I have led away, and they shall write it; and I shall also speak unto all nations of the earth and they shall write it.

13. And it shall come to pass that the Jews shall have the words of the Nephites, and the Nephites shall have the words of the Jews; and the Nephites and the Jews shall have the words of the lost tribes of Israel; and the lost tribes of Israel shall have the words of the Nephites and the Jews.

14. And it shall come to pass that my people, which are of the house of Israel, shall be gathered home unto the lands of their possessions; and my word also shall be gathered in one. And I will show unto them that fight against my word and against my people, who are of the house of Israel, that I am God, and that I covenanted with Abraham that I would remember his seed forever.

CHAPTER 30.

1. And now behold, my beloved brethren, I would speak unto you; for I, Nephi, would not suffer that ye should suppose that ye are more righteous than the Gentiles shall be. For behold, except ye shall keep the commandments of God ye shall all likewise perish; and because of the words which have been spoken ye need not suppose that the Gentiles are utterly destroyed.

2. For behold, I say unto you that as many of the Gentiles as will repent are the covenant people of the Lord; and as many of the Jews as will not repent shall be cast off; for the Lord covenanteth with none save it be with them that repent and believe in his Son, who is the Holy One of Israel.

3. And now, I would prophesy somewhat more

concerning the Jews and the Gentiles. For after the book of which I have spoken shall come forth, and be written unto the Gentiles, and sealed up again unto the Lord, there shall be many which shall believe the words which are written; and they shall carry them forth unto the remnant of our seed.

4. And then shall the remnant of our seed know concerning us, how that we came out from Jerusalem, and that they are descendants of the Jews.

5. And the gospel of Jesus Christ shall be declared among them; wherefore, they shall be restored unto the knowledge of their fathers, and also to the knowledge of Jesus Christ, which was had among their fathers.

6. And then shall they rejoice; for they shall know that it is a blessing unto them from the hand of God; and their scales of darkness shall begin to fall from their eyes; and many generations shall not pass away among them, save they shall be a white and delightsome people.

7. And it shall come to pass that the Jews which are scattered also shall begin to believe in Christ; and they shall begin to gather in upon the face of the land; and as many as shall believe in Christ shall also become a delightsome people.

8. And it shall come to pass that the Lord God shall commence his work among all nations, kindreds, tongues, and people, to bring about the restoration of his people upon the earth.

9. And with righteousness shall the Lord God judge the poor, and reprove with equity for the meek of the earth. And he shall smite the earth with the rod of his mouth; and with the breath of his lips shall he slay the wicked.

10. For the time speedily cometh that the Lord God shall cause a great division among the people, and the wicked will he destroy; and he will spare his people, yea, even if it so be that he must destroy the wicked by fire.

11. And righteousness shall be the girdle of his loins, and faithfulness the girdle of his reins.

12. And then shall the wolf dwell with the lamb; and the leopard shall lie down with the kid, and the calf, and the young lion, and the fatling, together; and a little child shall lead them.

13. And the cow and the bear shall feed; their young ones shall lie down together; and the lion shall eat straw like the ox.

14. And the sucking child shall play on the hole of the asp, and the weaned child shall put his hand on the cockatrice's den.

15. They shall not hurt nor destroy in all my holy mountain; for the earth shall be full of the knowledge of the Lord as the waters cover the sea.

16. Wherefore, the things of all nations shall be made known; yea, all things shall be made known unto the children of men.

17. There is nothing which is secret save it shall be revealed; there is no work of darkness save it shall be made manifest in the light; and there is nothing which is sealed upon the earth save it shall be loosed.

18. Wherefore, all things which have been revealed unto the children of men shall at that day be revealed; and Satan shall have power over the hearts of the children of men no more, for a long time. And now, my beloved brethren, I must make an end of my sayings.

CHAPTER 31.

1. And now I, Nephi, make an end of my prophesying unto you, my beloved brethren. And I cannot write but a few things, which I know must surely come to pass; neither can I write but a few of the words of my brother Jacob.

2. Wherefore, the things which I have written sufficeth me, save it be a few words which I must speak concerning the doctrine of Christ; wherefore, I shall speak unto you plainly, according to the plainness of my prophesying.

3. For my soul delighteth in plainness; for after this manner doth the Lord God work among the children of men. For the Lord God giveth light unto the understanding; for he speaketh unto men according to their language, unto their understanding.

4. Wherefore, I would that ye should remember that I have spoken unto you concerning that prophet which the Lord showed unto me, that should baptize the Lamb of God, which should take away the sins of the world.

5. And now, if the Lamb of God, he being holy, should have need to be baptized by water, to fulfil all righteousness, O then, how much more need have we, being unholy, to be baptized, yea, even by water!

6. And now, I would ask of you, my beloved brethren, wherein the Lamb of God did fulfil all righteousness in being baptized by water?

7. Know ye not that he was holy? But notwithstanding he being holy, he showeth unto the children of men that, according to the flesh he humbleth himself before the Father, and witnesseth unto the Father that he would be obedient unto him in keeping his commandments.

8. Wherefore, after he was baptized with water the Holy Ghost descended upon him in the form of a dove.

9. And again, it showeth unto the children of men the straightness of the path, and the narrowness of the gate, by which they should enter, he having set the example before them.

10. And he said unto the children of men: Follow thou me. Wherefore, my beloved brethren, can we follow Jesus save we shall be willing to keep the commandments of the Father?

11. And the Father said: Repent ye, repent ye, and be baptized in the name of my Beloved Son.

12. And also, the voice of the Son came unto me, saying: He that is baptized in my name, to him will the Father give the Holy Ghost, like unto me; wherefore, follow me, and do the things which ye have seen me do.

13. Wherefore, my beloved brethren, I know that if ye shall follow the Son, with full purpose of heart, acting no hypocrisy and no deception before God, but with real intent, repenting of your sins, witnessing unto the Father that ye are willing to take upon you the name of Christ, by baptism—yea, by following your Lord and your Savior down into the water, according to his word, behold, then shall ye receive the Holy Ghost; yea, then cometh the baptism of fire and of the Holy Ghost; and then can ye speak with the tongue of angels, and shout praises unto the Holy One of Israel.

14. But, behold, my beloved brethren, thus came the voice of the Son unto me, saying: After ye have repented of your sins, and witnessed unto the Father that ye are willing to keep my commandments, by the baptism of water, and have received the baptism of fire and of the Holy Ghost, and can speak with a new tongue, yea, even with the tongue of angels, and after this should deny me, it would have been better for you that ye had not known me.

15. And I heard a voice from the Father, saying: Yea, the words of my Beloved are true and faithful. He that endureth to the end, the same shall be saved.

16. And now, my beloved brethren, I know by this that unless a man shall endure to the end, in following the example of the Son of the living God, he cannot be saved.

17. Wherefore, do the things which I have told you I have seen that your Lord and your Redeemer should do; for, for this cause have they been shown unto me, that ye might know the gate by which ye should enter. For the gate by which ye should enter is repentance and baptism by water; and then cometh a remission of your sins by fire and by the Holy Ghost.

18. And then are ye in this straight and narrow path which leads to eternal life; yea, ye have entered in by the gate; ye have done according to the commandments of

the Father and the Son; and ye have received the Holy Ghost, which witnesses of the Father and the Son, unto the fulfilling of the promise which he hath made, that if ye entered in by the way ye should receive.

19. And now, my beloved brethren, after ye have gotten into this straight and narrow path, I would ask if all is done? Behold, I say unto you, Nay; for ye have not come thus far save it were by the word of Christ with unshaken faith in him, relying wholly upon the merits of him who is mighty to save.

20. Wherefore, ye must press forward with a steadfastness in Christ, having a perfect brightness of hope, and a love of God and of all men. Wherefore, if ye shall press forward, feasting upon the word of Christ, and endure to the end, behold, thus saith the Father: Ye shall have eternal life.

21. And now, behold, my beloved brethren, this is the way; and there is none other way nor name given under heaven whereby man can be saved in the kingdom of God. And now, behold, this is the doctrine of Christ, and the only and true doctrine of the Father, and of the Son, and of the Holy Ghost, which is one God, without end. Amen.

CHAPTER 32.

1. And now, behold, my beloved brethren, I suppose that ye ponder somewhat in your hearts concerning that which ye should do after ye have entered in by the way. But, behold, why do ye ponder these things in your hearts?

2. Do ye not remember that I said unto you that after ye had received the Holy Ghost ye could speak with the tongue of angels? And now, how could ye speak with the tongue of angels save it were by the Holy Ghost?

3. Angels speak by the power of the Holy Ghost; wherefore, they speak the words of Christ. Wherefore, I said unto you, feast upon the words of Christ; for behold, the words of Christ will tell you all things what ye should do.

4. Wherefore, now after I have spoken these words, if ye cannot understand them it will be because ye ask not, neither do ye knock; wherefore, ye are not brought into the light, but must perish in the dark.

5. For behold, again I say unto you that if ye will enter in by the way, and receive the Holy Ghost, it will show unto you all things what ye should do.

6. Behold, this is the doctrine of Christ, and there will be no more doctrine given until after he shall manifest himself unto you in the flesh. And when he shall manifest

himself unto you in the flesh, the things which he shall say unto you shall ye observe to do.

7. And now I, Nephi, cannot say more; the Spirit stoppeth mine utterance, and I am left to mourn because of the unbelief, and the wickedness, and the ignorance, and the stiffneckedness of men; for they will not search knowledge, nor understand great knowledge, when it is given unto them in plainness, even as plain as word can be.

8. And now, my beloved brethren, I perceive that ye ponder still in your hearts; and it grieveth me that I must speak concerning this thing. For if ye would hearken unto the Spirit which teacheth a man to pray ye would know that ye must pray; for the evil spirit teacheth not a man to pray, but teacheth him that he must not pray.

9. But behold, I say unto you that ye must pray always, and not faint; that ye must not perform any thing unto the Lord save in the first place ye shall pray unto the Father in the name of Christ, that he will consecrate thy performance unto thee, that thy performance may be for the welfare of thy soul.

CHAPTER 33.

1. And now I, Nephi, cannot write all the things which were taught among my people; neither am I mighty in writing, like unto speaking; for when a man speaketh by the power of the Holy Ghost the power of the Holy Ghost carrieth it unto the hearts of the children of men.

2. But behold, there are many that harden their hearts against the Holy Spirit, that it hath no place in them; wherefore, they cast many things away which are written and esteem them as things of naught.

3. But I, Nephi, have written what I have written, and I esteem it as of great worth, and especially unto my people. For I pray continually for them by day, and mine eyes water my pillow by night, because of them; and I cry unto my God in faith, and I know that he will hear my cry.

4. And I know that the Lord God will consecrate my prayers for the gain of my people. And the words which I have written in weakness will be made strong unto them; for it persuadeth them to do good; it maketh known unto them of their fathers; and it speaketh of Jesus, and persuadeth them to believe in him, and to endure to the end, which is life eternal.

5. And it speaketh harshly against sin, according to the plainness of the truth; wherefore, no man will be angry at the words which I have written save he shall be

of the spirit of the devil.

6. I glory in plainness; I glory in truth; I glory in my Jesus, for he hath redeemed my soul from hell.

7. I have charity for my people, and great faith in Christ that I shall meet many souls spotless at his judgment-seat.

8. I have charity for the Jew—I say Jew, because I mean them from whence I came.

9. I also have charity for the Gentiles. But behold, for none of these can I hope except they shall be reconciled unto Christ, and enter into the narrow gate, and walk in the straight path which leads to life, and continue in the path until the end of the day of probation.

10. And now, my beloved brethren, and also Jew, and all ye ends of the earth, hearken unto these words and believe in Christ; and if ye believe not in these words believe in Christ. And if ye shall believe in Christ ye will believe in these words, for they are the words of Christ, and he hath given them unto me; and they teach all men that they should do good.

11. And if they are not the words of Christ, judge ye—for Christ will show unto you, with power and great glory, that they are his words, at the last day; and you and I shall stand face to face before his bar; and ye shall know that I have been commanded of him to write these things, notwithstanding my weakness.

12. And I pray the Father in the name of Christ that many of us, if not all, may be saved in his kingdom at that great and last day.

13. And now, my beloved brethren, all those who are of the house of Israel, and all ye ends of the earth, I speak unto you as the voice of one crying from the dust: Farewell until that great day shall come.

14. And you that will not partake of the goodness of God, and respect the words of the Jews, and also my words, and the words which shall proceed forth out of the mouth of the Lamb of God, behold, I bid you an everlasting farewell, for these words shall condemn you at the last day.

15. For what I seal on earth, shall be brought against you at the judgment bar; for thus hath the Lord commanded me, and I must obey. Amen.

Moroni's Challenge

And when ye shall receive these things, I would exhort you that ye would ask God, the Eternal Father, in the name of Christ, if these things are not true; and if ye shall ask with a sincere heart, with real intent, having faith in Christ, he will manifest the truth of it unto you, by the power of the Holy Ghost. Moroni 10:4.

E wish to express our deep appreciation to The First Presidency of The Church of Jesus Christ of Latter-day Saints for their allowing us to use, in this publication, the text of the Book of Mormon. We print here only the text for that part covered by the illustrations. Subsequent volumes will contain the text for the parts each volume covers.

We do not print here any other material found in various copyrighted editions of the Book of Mormon, such as the prefatory material and other writings found prior to the First Book of Nephi.

— *The Publishers*

PREVIEW OF VOLUME V

We feel you will enjoy this next volume which covers the writings of Jacob, brother of Nephi, Enos, Jarom and Omni, as well as other writers during the 414 years covered in this volume.

You will enjoy Mormon's explanation of the makeup of his record and the connection between the Large and Small Plates of Nephi.